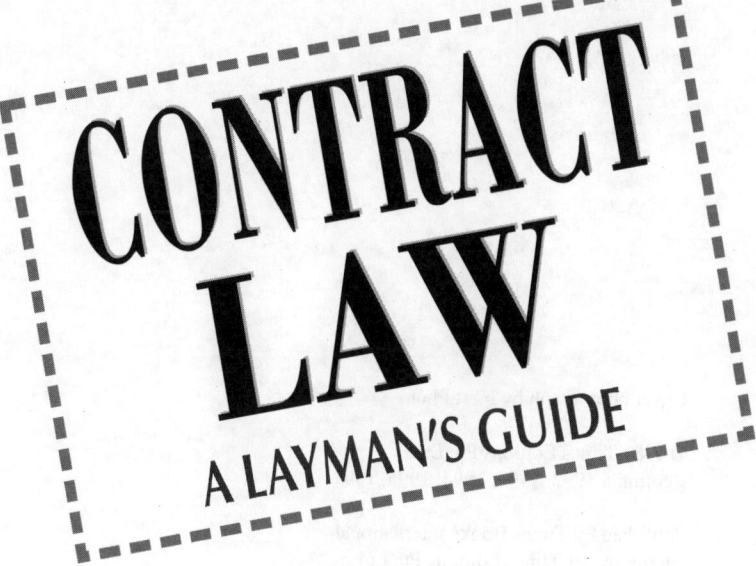

Catherine Tay Swee Kian
LL.B. (Hons.)(London); LL.M(London);
of Lincoln's Inn, Barrister-at-law;
Advocate and Solicitor of the Supreme Court of Singapore;
Senior Lecturer in Law, National University of Singapore.

and

Tang See Chim
B.Sc (Econ.)(Hons.)(London);
of the Middle Temple, Barrister-at-law;
Advocate and Solicitor of the Supreme Court of Singapore.

With a Foreword by
The former Chief Justice Wee Chong Jin

TIMES BOOKS INTERNATIONAL
Singapore • Kuala Lumpur

Cover photograph by First Photo

© 1987 Times Editions Pte Ltd
Reprinted 1992, 1993, 1994, 1995, 1997

Published by Times Books International
An imprint of Times Editions Pte Ltd
Times Centre
1 New Industrial Road
Singapore 536196
Tel: (65) 284 8844
Fax: (65) 285 4871
e-mail: te@corp.tpl.com.sg

Times Subang
Lot 46, Subang Hi-Tech Industrial Park
Batu Tiga
40000 Shah Alam
Selangor Darul Ehsan
Malaysia
Tel and Fax: (603) 736 3517

All rights reserved. No part of this publication may be reproduced or transmitted in any form or by any means, electronic or mechanical, including photocopying, recording or any information storage or retrieval system, without written permission from the publisher.

Printed by CMO Image Printing Enterprise

ISBN 981 204 143 5

*To friendship
and cooperation*

Foreword

In the Preface the authors say

"This book seeks to outline the law of contract in simple language, language intelligible to the general reader. We hope the book will give him a better understanding of the consequences of his dealings with other people in his everyday life."

I congratulate the authors on having, I believe, achieved their objective. The general reader who reads this book with the object of acquiring a general knowledge of the law of contract, a branch of law which touches his daily actions, will find it written in simple, easily understandable language and extremely useful and helpful.

I believe this book will also be well received by law students as a helpful general introduction to the law of contract and by legal practitioners as a quick and useful reference material on any particular aspect of contract law.

WEE CHONG JIN
The former Chief Justice
of Singapore

Preface

One normally thinks of a contract as a commercial transaction that only affects the businessman. Nothing is further from the truth. The law of contract affects one's everyday life.

You lose your pet dog. You post a reward for its return. Someone finds it and returns it. You are too happy to be reunited with your lost dog to ask whether the person returning it is entitled, in law, to the reward. Indeed you believe you are under a moral obligation to hand over the reward, whatever the law may say.

But what does the law say? In law, it depends on whether the person returning the dog knows of the reward when he returns it. If he does, he is entitled to the reward. If he does not, he is not.

You may ask why? This is because of a technical rule in the law of contract relating to offer and acceptance. For there to be a contract there must be an offer (here, the reward) by one party and acceptance of the offer (here, the return of the dog) by the other party. But an offer cannot be accepted by a person who is ignorant of it.

But can he demand the reward now that he knows of it? No, says the law. Why? Because there is no consideration. The return of the dog without knowledge of the reward is a gratuitous act (ie, an act without consideration) which the law does not lend its authority to enforce. The law enforces only binding bargains.

What constitutes binding bargains, the forms they take and their legal consequences are the subject matters of this book.

What a contract is is defined in Chapter 1. Chapters 2, 3 and 4 discuss the essential elements (offer and acceptance, consideration, intention to create legal relations) without which there can be no contract. Chapter 5 examines the forms of a contract while Chapter 6 enquires into the capacity of different classes of persons to make contracts and the legal effects of contracts made by them. The terms of contract are considered in Chapter 7 and exemption clauses in Chapter 8. A contract may be void or voidable because of misrepresentation (Chapter 9); duress and undue influence (Chapter 10); mistake (Chapter 11) and illegality (Chapter 12). A contract is discharged by performance or breach (Chapter 13); and the remedies for breach are discussed in Chapter 14. The last chapter offers some useful tips on how to draft a contract.

This book seeks to outline the law of contract in simple language, language intelligible to the general reader. We hope the book will give him a better understanding of the consequences of his dealings with other people in his everyday life.

We are grateful to the former Chief Justice, Mr Wee Chong Jin, for writing the Foreword. His kindness and encouragement should spur us on to further writing on the law for the general reader. We are also grateful to our publishers for bringing out this book so soon after our last book, *Your Rights as a Consumer—A Guide to Sale of Goods • Hire-purchase • Small Claims Tribunals*.

The law is stated as at Febuary 1991.

Catherine Tay Swee Kian

Tang See Chim

Abbreviations

CLA	— Civil Law Act (Cap. 30)
FCA	— Frustrated Contracts Act (Cap. 33)
IRA	— Infants Relief Act 1874 (UK)
MA	— Misrepresentation Act 1967 (UK)
MCA	— Minor's Contracts Act 1987 (UK)
SGA	— Sale of Goods Act 1979 (UK)
SF	— Statute of Frauds 1677 (UK)
UCTA	— Unfair Contract Terms Act 1977 (UK)

Contents

Foreword 5
Preface 6
Abbreviations 8
Table of Cases 13
Table of Statutes 18

Chapter 1 – Nature and Definition of Contract
   1. Reception of English Law in Singapore 19
   2. What is a Contract? 19

Chapter 2 – Formation of Contract
   1. Agreement 20
   2. Invitation to Treat 20
   3. The Offer 21
   4. Communication of Offer 22
   5. Revocation of Offer 22
   6. Rejection of Offer 23
   7. Lapse of Offer 23
   8. The Acceptance 24
   9. Absolute and Unqualified Acceptance 24
   10. Counter-offer 24
   11. Request for Information 25
   12. Correspondence constituting Contract 26
   13. Communication of Acceptance 27
   14. Cross-offers 29
   15. Acceptance Subject to Contract 30
   16. The Agreement 30

Chapter 3 – Intention to Create Legal Relations
   1. Domestic and Social Agreements 31
   2. Commercial Agreements 33

Chapter 4 – Consideration
1. What is Consideration? 35
2. Types of Consideration 35
3. Rules on Consideration 37
   a. Consideration required for all Simple Contracts 37
   b. Consideration must be Sufficient or Real but need not be Adequate 37
   c. Consideration must be Legal 38
   d. Consideration must not be Past 38
   e. Consideration must Move from the Promisee/ Plaintiff 38
   f. Consideration must be for Something which the Promisor is already bound to do 38
   g. Rule in Pinnel's Case - Part Payment of a Debt is no Consideration for Discharge of the Whole Debt 39
4. Promissory Estoppel 41

Chapter 5 – Form of Contract
1. Contracts under Seal or by Deed 43
2. Contracts which must be in Writing 43
3. Contracts which must be Evidenced in Writing 44
4. Doctrine of Part Performance 45
5. No Formalities Required 47
6. Minor's Contracts Act 47

Chapter 6 – Capacity
1. Minors 48
   a. Valid Contracts 48
   b. Voidable Contracts 50
   c. Void Contracts 50
2. Corporations 51
3. Mentally Disordered and Drunken Persons 52

Chapter 7 – Terms of the Contract
1. Terms and Representations 53
2. Terms of Contract 54
3. Express Terms 54
4. Implied Terms 54
5. Conditions and Warranties 56

Chapter 8 – Exemption Clauses
1. Judicial Restrictions 59
2. Statutory Restrictions 63
3. Fundamental Breach and Exemption Clause 64

Chapter 9 – Misrepresentation
1. What is Misrepresentation? 67
2. Silence as Misrepresentation 68
3. Inducement 70
4. Misrepresentation need not be Sole Inducement 70
5. Effect of Misrepresentation 71
6. Types of Misrepresentation 71
7. Fraudulent Misrepresentation 72
8. Negligent Misrepresentation 73
9. Innocent Misrepresentation 75
10. Rescission 75
11. Restitution and Indemnity 75
12. Loss of Right to Rescind 76
13. Misrepresentation and Breach 77
14. Misrepresentation and Exemption Clauses 78

Chapter 10 – Duress and Undue Influence
1. (A) Duress 79
   (B) Economic Duress 79
2. Undue Influence 80
3. Right to Relief Lost 82

Chapter 11 – Mistake
1. Common Mistake 83
2. Mutual Mistake 85
3. Unilateral Mistake 86
4. Mistake over Documents 89
5. Rectification of Written Agreements 91

Chapter 12 – Illegal Contracts
1. Contracts Prohibited by Statute 92
2. Contracts Illegal at Common Law 92
3. Consequences of Illegal Contracts 94
4. Void Contracts 95
5. Restraint in a Contract of Employment 97

6. Restraint in a Contract of Sale of Business 99
7. Solus Trading Agreements 99

Chapter 13 – Discharge of Contracts
1. Discharge by Performance 101
2. Discharge by Agreement 104
3. Discharge by Frustration 105
4. Limits to Doctrine of Frustration 107
5. Effect of Frustration 108
6. Discharge by Breach 109

Chapter 14 – Remedies for Breach of Contract
1. Refusal of Further Performance 113
2. Damages 113
3. Remoteness of Damage 114
4. Measure of Damages 116
5. Speculative Damages 117
6. Mitigation 117
7. Liquidated Damages 118
8. Quantum Meruit 120
9. Specific Performance 120
10. Injunction 122

Chapter 15 – How to Draft a Contract?
1. General Principles 123
2. Drafting Rules 124
3. Intelligibility of Contract Documents 125
4. Use of Precedents 125
5. Drafting in Paragraphs 125
6. Use of Descriptive Words 126
7. Habits You Should Avoid 126
8. Schedules 128
9. Check Your Draft 128
10. Specimen Agreement 129

Appendix 130

The Authors 132

Index 133

Table of Cases

Adam v Lindsell (1818) I B & AId. 681 29
Alder Dickson [1955] 1 Q.B. 158 63
Alderslade v Hendon Laundry [1945] K.B. 189 60
Allcard v Skinner (1887) 36 Ch. D. 145 82
Atlas Express Ltd v Kafco (Importers & Distributors) Ltd [1989} 1 All. E.R. 641 80
Attwood v Small (1838) 6 Cf. & Fin. 232 70
Avery v Bowden (1885) 5 E. & B. 714 111
Balfour v Balfour [1919] 2 K.B. 571 32
Bell v Lever Bros [1932] A.C. 161 84
Bettini v Gye (1876) 1 Q.B.D. 183 56
Bisset v Wilkinson [1927] A.C. 177 67
British Concrete Co v Schelff [1921] 2 Ch. 563 99
Byrne v Tienhoven (1880) 5 C.P.D. 344 23
Car & Universal Finance Co Ltd v Caldwell [1961] 1 Q.B. 525 75
Carlill v Carbolic Smoke Ball Co. [1892] 2 Q.B.484 21,22
Central London Property Trust Ltd v High Trees House Ltd [1947] K.B. 130 42
Chalmers v Harding (1868) 17 L.T.S 71 68
Chapelton v Barry UDC [1940] 1 K.B. 532 59
Chaplin v Hicks [1911] 2 K.B. 786 117
Chappell & Co Ltd v Nestle Co Ltd [1960] A.C. 87 37
Chapple v Cooper (1844) 13 M. & W. 252 49
Chillingworth v Esche [1924] 1 Ch. 97 30
Combe v Combe [1951] 2 K.B. 215 42

Condor v Barron Knights [1966] 1 W.L.R
87 106
Couturier v Hastie (1856) 5 H.L.C. 673 83
Coutts & Co v Browne-Lecky [1947] K.B.
104 51
Cumming v Ince (1847) 11 Q.B. 112 79
Cundy v Lindsay (1878) 3 App. Cas. 459 87
Curries v Misa (1875) L.R. 10 Ex 153 35
Curtis v Chemical Cleaning Co [1951] 1
K.B. 805 60
Cutter v Powell (1795) 6 Term. Rep. 320 101
Davis Contractors v Fareham UDC [1956]
A.C. 696 108
De Bernardy v Harding (1853) 8 Exch.822 120
Derry v Peek (1889) 14 App. Cas. 337 72
Dickinson v Dodds (1876) 2 Ch.D. 463 23
Dunlop Pneumatic Tyre Co Ltd v
New Garage & Motor Co Ltd [1915]
A.C. 79 119
Edgington v Fitzmaurice (1885) 29 Ch. D.
459 .... 68, 70
Entores v Miles Far East Corporation
(1955) 2 All E.R. 493 27
Esso Petroleum Co v Harper's Garage
[1968] A.C. 269 100
Fisher v Bell (1960) 3 All E.R. 731 21
Fitch v Dewes [1921] 2 A.C. 158 98
Foakes v Beer (1884) 9 App. Cas. 605 40
Foster v Mackinnon (1869) L.R. 4 C.P.
704 91
Foster v Suggett (1918) 35 T.L.R. 87 98
Glasbrook Bros v Glamorgan County
Council [1925] A.C. 270. 39
Grist v Bailey [1967] Ch. 532 85
H Parsons (Livestock) v Uttley Ingham
[1978] Q.B. 791 116
Hadley v Baxendale (1854) 9 Exch. 341 114
Hedley Byrne & Co Ltd v Heller &
Partners Ltd [1964] A.C. 465 73
Henthorn v Fraser [1892] 2 Ch. 27 28

Hirachand Punamchand v Temple [1911]
2 K.B. 330 41
Hochster v De La Tour (1853) 2
E. & B. 678 111
Hoenig V Issacs [1952] 2 All E.R. 176 104
Household Fire Insurance Co v Grant
1879) 4 Ex D. 216 28
Howel Securities v Hughes [1974] 1 All
E.R. 161 29
Hughes v Liverpool Victoria Legal
Friendly Society [1916] 2 K.B. 95
Hyde v Wrench (1840) 3 Beav. 334 25
Imperial Loan Co v Stone [1892] 1 Q.B.
599 52
Ingram v Little [1961] 1 Q.B.31 89
Jarvis v Swan Tours [1973] Q.B. 233 117
Jones v Padavatton [1979] 2 All E.R. 166 32
Joscelyne v Nissen [1970] 2 Q.B. 86 91
King's Norton Metal Co Ltd v Edridge,
Merrett & Co Ltd (1897) 14 T.L.R. 98 87
Klinewort Benson v Malaysia Mining Corp.
Bhd [1989] 1 All E.R. 785 34
Krell v Henry [1903] 2 K.B. 740 106
L'Estrange v Graucob [1934] 2 K.B. 394 59
Lai Kwee Lan & Anor v Ng Kew Lay
& Anor [1990] 1 M.L.J. 211 80
Leaf v International Galleries [1950] 2
K.B. 86 76
Les Affreteurs Reunis Societe Anonyme v
Walford [1919] A.C. 801 55
Leslie v Sheill [1914] 3 K.B. 607 51
Lewis v Avery [1972] 1 Q.B. 198 88
Lloyds bank v Bundy [1975] Q.B. 326 82
Maddison v Alderson (1883) 8 App. Cas.
467 46
Maritime National Fish v Ocean Trawlers
[1935] A.C. 524 107
Merritt v Merritt [1970] 1 W.L.R. 1211 32
Moorcock (1889) 14 P.D. 64 55
Nash v Inman [1908] 2 K.B. 1 49
Ng Bros. Construction v Kaolin (M)
Sdn Bhd [1985] 1 M.L.J. 245 24

Olley v Marlborough Court [1949] 1 K.B. 532 61
Page One Records Ltd v Britton [1967] 3 All E.R. 822 122
Panachand & Co (Pte) Ltd v Riko International Pte Ltd [1986] 1 M.L.J. 294 105
Parker v S E Railway (1877) 2 C.P.D. 416 61
Parkinson v College of Ambulance Ltd [1925] 2 K.B. 1 93
Pearce v Brooks (1866) L.R. 1 Ex 213 93
Pearce v Gardner [1897] 1 Q.B. 688 44
Pharmaceutical Society of Great Britain v Boots Cash Chemists (Southern) Ltd [1953] 1 Q.B. 401 21
Phillips v Brooks [1919] 2 K.B. 243 88
Photo Production Ltd v Securicor Transport Ltd (1980) A.C. 827 65
Pilkington v Wood [1953] Ch. 770 118
Planche v Colburn (1831) 8 Bing. 14 103
Poussard v Spiers(1876)1 Q.B.D.410 56
Pym v Campbell (1856) 6 E. & B. 370 54
R v Clarke (1927) 40 C.L.R. 227 22
Raffles v Wichelhaus (1864) 2 H.& C.906 86
Ramsgate Victoria Hotel Co v Montefiore (1866) L.R. 1 Ex. 109 24
Re Shipton [1915] 3 K.B. 676 107
Redgrave v Hurd (1881) 20 Ch. D. 1 70
Roberts v Gray [1913] 1 K.B. 520 50
Roberts v Havelock (1832) 102
Roscorla v Thomas [1842] 3 Q.B. 234 38
Rose and Frank v J.R. Crompton & Bros [1923] 2 K.B. 261 .... 31, 33
Ryan v Mutual Tontine Westminster Chambers Association (1893) 1 Ch. 116 121
Salomon v Salomon & Co Ltd [1897] A.C. 22 52
Saunders v Anglia Building Society [1971] A.C. 1004 90
Scriven Bros v Hindley & Co [1913] 3 K.B. 564 86

Simpkins v Pays [1955] 1 W.L.R. 975 33
Smith v Land & House Property
 Corporation (1884) 28 Ch. D.7 68
Solle v Butcher [1950] 1 K.B. 671 85
Spurling v Bradshaw [1956] 2 All E.R. 121 62
Stevenson v McLean (1880)5 Q.B.D.346 26
Stilk v Myrick (1809) 2 Camp. 317 39
Suisse Atlantique (1967) 1 A.C. 361 64
Sumpter v Hedges [1898] 1 Q.B. 673 103
Tan Geok Khoon & Gerard Francis Robless
 v Paya Terubong Estate Sdn. Bhd.
 [1988] 2 M.L.J. 672 26
Taylor v Caldwell (1836) 3 B. & S. 826 106
The Heron II (Czarnikow v Koufos) [1969]
 1 A.C. 350 115
The Mihalis Angelos [1971] 1 O.B. 164 112
Thorton v Shoe Lane Parking [1971]
 2 Q.B.163 62
Tinn v Hoffmann & Co (1873) 29 L.T. 271 30
Tsakiroglou & Co v Noblee and Thor
 G.m.b.H. [1962] A.C. 93 108
Upfill v Wright [1911] 1 K.B. 506 93
Victoria Laundry (Windsor) v Newman
 Industries [1949] 2 K.B. 528 115
Wakeham v Mackenzie [1969] 2 All E.R.
 783 46
Warner Bros v Nelson [1937] 1 K.B. 209 122
White & Carter (Councils) v McGregor
 [1962] A.C. 413 112
Whittingon v Seale-Hayne (1900) 82 L.T.
 49 76
With v O'Flanagon [1936]Ch.575 69

Table of Statutes

Civil Law Act (Cap. 30)
Section
    5.. 19,48
Conveyancing and Law of Property Act (Cap. 268)
Section
    53... 44
Evidence Act (Cap 97)
Section
    113..81
Family Law Reform Act 1969 (UK).. 48
Frustrated Contracts Act (Cap. 33)
Section
    2(2).. 109
    2(3).. 109
    3(5).. 109
Infants Relief Act 1874 (UK)... 50
Minors Contracts Act 1987 (UK)
Section
    3..47
Misrepresentation Act 1967 (UK)
Section
    2...74
Sale of Goods Act 1979 (UK)
Section
    3... 50, 52
    12..63
Statute of Frauds 1677 (UK)
Section
    4..44
Unfair Contract Terms Act 1977 (UK)
Section
    6..63

1 Nature and Definition of Contract

1. Reception of English Law in Singapore
English law as modified by local conditions is a source of commercial law in Singapore. Contract law is part of commercial law. With regard to contracts, English law is applicable by virtue of the Second Charter of Justice 1826 and also by virtue of section 5(1) of the Civil Law Act. Cap 30.

2. What is a Contract?
A contract is an agreement which binds the parties concerned. In other words, a contract is an agreement which is enforceable by law.

To have an agreement, there must be an offer and an acceptance of that offer.

$$\text{Offer} + \text{Acceptance} = \text{Agreement}$$

To have a contract, certain essential elements must be present. These are:
— agreement (offer and acceptance);
— intention to create legal relations;
— consideration; and
— capacity.

These essential elements will be discussed in the following chapters. The contract must not, of course, be affected by circumstances which render the contract unenforceable, voidable (ie, capable of being set aside), void or illegal.

$$\text{Agreement} + \text{Consideration} + \text{Intention to create Legal Relations} + \text{Capacity} = \text{Contract}$$

2 Formation of Contract

1. Agreement
The essence of contract is that there should be an agreement. Parties to a contract must first reach an agreement. To have an agreement, there should be an offer by one party which is accepted by the other party.

2. Invitation to Treat
An offer must be distinguished from an invitation to treat (ie, an invitation to make an offer). An invitation to treat is not an offer which is capable of being turned into a contract by acceptance. An invitation to treat is a mere invitation by one party to the other party to make an offer. An invitation to treat is usually found in advertisements in newspapers and shop window displays. A good example is the display of goods in a self-service supermarket.

Illustration
A shopkeeper displaying goods on his shelves with a price tag on them is not making an offer. He is merely inviting the public to make an offer to buy the goods at the price stated. It is an invitation to treat and therefore is not capable of being accepted. If a customer tenders the price and demands the goods the shopkeeper is not bound to sell them to him. The demand of the customer is the offer which the shopkeeper is free to accept or reject. So advertisements like "special offer" or "clearance sale" are not offers in the legal sense.

In an auction the auctioneer invites bidders to make an offer. Acceptance of the offer is indicated by the fall of the hammer.

Pharmaceutical Society of Great Britain v Boots Cash Chemists (Southern) Ltd[1]

The facts were as follows:
> Goods were sold in B's shop under the self-service system. Customers selected their purchases from shelves on which goods were displayed, put them into a basket and took them to the cash desk where they paid the price.
> *Held:* the contract was made, not when the customer put the goods in the basket but when the cashier accepted the offer to buy and received the payment. The display of such goods on the shelves was an invitation to treat. An offer was made by the customer when he presented the goods at at the cash desk. The customer's offer could be accepted or rejected by the cashier.

Fisher v Bell[2]

The facts were as follows:
> B displayed in his shop window a flick-knife behind which was a ticket bearing the words, "Ejector knife - 4 shillings". B was charged with offering for sale a flick-knife, contrary to the provisions of the Restriction of Offensive Weapons Act.
> *Held:* the displaying of the flick-knife was merely an invitation to treat. Hence, there was no offer for sale and B could not be guilty of the offence.

3. The Offer

The offer may be expressed or implied by conduct. The person making the offer is called the offeror. The person to whom it is made is called the offeree. For example, A offers to sell his car to B for $10,000. A is the ofteror. B is the offeree.

An offer may be made to a definite person, or to some definite class of persons or to the world at large. An offer to a definite person can only be accepted by that person. An offer to some definite class can only be accepted by a member of that class. An offer to the world at large can be accepted by anyone. This can be illustrated by the famous case of Carlill v

---

1. [1953] 1 Q.B. 401
2. (1960) 3 All E.R. 731

Carbolic Smoke Ball Co.[3] The facts were as follows:
> The defendants who were the proprietors of a medical preparation called "the Carbolic Smoke Ball" issued an advertisement in which they offered to pay £100 to any person who contracted influenza after having used one of their smoke balls in a specified manner and for a specified period. To show their sincerity, they deposited a sum of £1,000 with their bankers. On the faith of the advertisement, the plaintiff bought and used the ball as prescribed but notwithstanding that she contracted influenza. She sued for the £100.
>
> *Held:* the company was bound to pay. It is an offer made to all the world; and would ripen into a contract with anybody coming forward and performing the condition.

4. Communication of Offer

An offer must be communicated to the offeree before it can be accepted. The offeree cannot accept an offer unless he knows of it. In other words, the offeree cannot intend to accept an offer of which he is ignorant.

Illustration

Suppose K offers by advertisement a reward of $100 to anyone who returns his lost dog and Y finds the dog and returns it to K without having heard of the offer of reward, Y is not entitled to $100.

In the case of R v Clarke,[4] the facts were as follows:
> The Government of Western Australia offered a reward of £1,000 for information leading to the arrest and conviction of the murderers of 2 police officers. C saw the offer but forgot it and later gave the necessary information.
>
> *Held:* C was not entitled to the reward.

5. Revocation of Offer

An offer may be revoked at any time before acceptance. An offer is irrevocable after acceptance. Revocation of offer is

---

3. [1892] 2 Q.B. 484
4. (1927) 40 C.L.R. 227

Formation of Contract

not effective until it is actually communicated to the offeree. Communication means that the revocation must have actually reached the offeree.

In the case of Byrne v Van Tienhoven,[5] the facts were as follows:
> A by letter of 1 October offered to sell goods to B in New York. B received the offer on the 11th and immediately telegraphed his acceptance. On the 8th, A wrote revoking his offer and this reached B on the 20th.
> *Held:* the revocation was of no effect until it reached B and a contract was made when B telegraphed.

The communication of revocation need not be made by the offeror. It is sufficient that the offeree learns of the revocation from a reliable source. The case of Dickinson v Dodds[6] illustrates this point. The facts were as follows:
> X agreed to sell property to Y by a document which stated "this offer to be left over until Friday, 9 am". On Thursday X contracted to sell the property to Z. Y heard of this from B and on Friday at 7 am he delivered to X an acceptance of his offer.
> *Held:* Y could not accept X's offer after he knew it had been revoked by the sale of the property to Z.

6. Rejection of Offer
An offer is rejected if:
— the offeree communicates his rejection to the offeror;
— the assent of the offeree is qualified or is subject to conditions imposed by him.

7. Lapse of Offer
An offer lapses:
(a) on the death either of the offeror or the offeree before acceptance;
(b) by non-acceptance within the time specified for acceptance by the offeror;
(c) by non-acceptance within a reasonable time when

---
5. (1880) 5 C.P.D. 344
6. (1876) 2 Ch. D. 463

no time for acceptance is specified. What a reasonable time is depends on the circumstances of the case.

This point was discussed in Ramsgate Victoria Hotel Co v Montefiore,[7] the facts of which were as follows:

M offered, on 8 June, to take shares in R company. M heard nothing until 23 November when he received a letter of acceptance. M refused to take the shares.

Held: M was entitled to refuse because his offer had lapsed before 23 November and thus could not be accepted. The offer lapses because the offeree is regarded as having refused it if he has not accepted it within a reasonable time.

8. The Acceptance

An agreement comes into existence when an offer is accepted. The acceptance must be made while the offer is still in force, ie, before it has lapsed, been revoked or rejected. Acceptance is thus only possible if the offer is still in force. Once the acceptance is completed, the offer becomes irrevocable.

Ng Bros. Construction v Kaolin (M) Sdn Bhd[8]

The Defendants, Kaolin, asked the Plaintiffs, Ng Bros. to submit a quotation for a clay factory complex. The Plaintiffs submitted a quotation which was then accepted by the Defendants on December 27 1969 in the following terms:

"We are pleased to inform you that we have accepted your quotation and therefore you may treat this letter as our official order to you."

However the letter also went on to say,

"We would also be sending you at a later date an official contract agreement for you to sign to complete the usual formality."

Held: The quotation was an offer and the letter of December 27 was an acceptance of it which created a binding contract between both parties. Consequently,

---

7. (1866) L.R. 1 Ex. 109
8. [1985] 1 M.L.J. 245

any subsequent disagreement could not affect the contract. In holding this view the Court of Appeal in Malaysia overruled the Sessions Court decision that the quotation was not an offer. The reference to "an official contract agreement" did not mean that there was no valid agreement concluded or that the contract would be rendered null and void at the instance of a party withdrawing its agreement to any terms which had been agreed upon.

9. Absolute and Unqualified Acceptance

An acceptance must be absolute and unqualified. Acceptance must conform exactly with the terms of the offer. If the offer requires an act to be done, the precise act and nothing else must be done. If the acceptance varies the terms of the offer, it is a counter-offer and not an acceptance of the original offer. A conditional acceptance is not an acceptance. For example, where goods are offered at a certain price, an assent coupled with a promise to pay by instalments is not an acceptance.

10. Counter-Offer

A counter-offer operates as a rejection of the original offer. Where an offeree makes a counter-offer, the original offer is deemed to have been rejected and cannot subsequently be accepted.

In the case of Hyde v Wrench,[9] the facts were as follows: On 6 June W offered to sell to H a farm for 1,000. H made a counter-offer of 950. On 27 June, W rejected the counter-offer. On 29 June H made a purported acceptance of the offer of 6 June.
Held: the counter-offer operated as a rejection of the original offer. There was no contract.

11. Request for Information

If, on receipt of an offer, the offeree requests the offeror to inform him whether he would be prepared to add a term to the offer, the offeree's request may be construed as a request for further information. In this case, since there is no counter-offer, the original offer remains open.

---

9. (1840) 3 Beav. 334

In the case of Stevenson v McLean,[10] the defendant offered to sell to the plaintiffs 3,800 tons of iron "at 40s net cash per ton, open till Monday". On Monday morning the plaintiffs telegraphed: "Please wire whether you would accept 40s for delivery over 2 months or if not, longest limit you would give". Having received no reply at 1.34 pm, the plaintiffs despatched a telegram accepting the original offer. At 1.25 pm the defendant despatched a telegram to say that he had sold the iron to a third party. This telegram did not reach the plaintiffs until some time after they had sent their telegram at 1.34 pm. The plaintiffs sued for breach of contract, contending that the defendant's offer was still open when they sent the telegram of acceptance. The defendant argued that the Monday morning telegram constituted a counter-offer.

It was held that the plaintiffs had not made a counter-offer but had made a mere enquiry which did not reject the offer. A binding contract had been made when the plaintiffs sent the telegram accepting the offer.

When a counter-offer is accepted, then its terms and not the terms of the original offer, become the terms of the contract.

12. Correspondence constituting Contract

In long drawn out negotiations where many letters were exchanged, it may not be clear when an offer was made and when such an offer was accepted. The courts will however be prepared to examine the documents and the correspondence exchanged between the parties to determine whether a contract was concluded.

Tan Geok Khoon & Gerard Francis Robless v Paya Terubong Estate Sdn Bhd.[11]
In that case, the judge examined a series of letters exchanged between the parties and upon their true construction, was able to find in such letters an offer and an acceptance of that offer and hence was able to hold that there was a contract concluded between the parties.

10. (1880) 5 Q.B.D. 346
11. [1988] 2 M.L.J. 672

13. Communication of Acceptance

The general rule is that the acceptance must be communicated to the offeror. Different rules apply to the communication of an acceptance in:
- (a) instantaneous contracts; and
- (b) contracts by post.

If the offeror prescribes a particular method of acceptance and the acceptor accepts in that way, there will be a contract. Failure to accept in the prescribed method means that there will be no contract. For example, K offers Y some iron, the acceptance to be made by telex. Y accepts by air-mail letter. That acceptance is ineffective because it did not comply with the terms of the offer.

The offeror may waive the requirement that acceptance be communicated, especially in unilateral contracts. The offer of a reward is a unilateral contract. If the offer is one which is to be accepted by being acted upon, no communication of the intention to accept is necessary, unless communication is stated in the offer itself. For example, if an offer of reward is made for finding a lost dog the offer is accepted by finding the dog. It is not necessary before searching for the dog to give notice of acceptance of the offer.

(a) Acceptance in Instantaneous Contracts

Instantaneous contracts mean contracts made between persons present or by telephone or telex. The contract is complete only when the acceptance is received by the offeror and not when transmitted. Acceptance takes place when it is actually brought to the notice of the offeror.

Illustration

Suppose K shouts an offer to Y across the river. K does not hear Y's reply because of the noise from a passing aeroplane. There is no effective acceptance.

In the case of Entores v Miles Far East Corporation,[12] an English company in London made an offer which was accepted by the Amsterdam company by telex. The court had to decide

---

12. (1955) 2 All E.R. 493

the time and place at which the contract was made: at Amsterdam where the acceptance was sent or in London where it was received. It was held that the contract was made in London where the notification of acceptance was received. Communication by telex was no different from cases where the parties were negotiating in the presence of each other.

(b) Acceptance by Post

Where contracts are made by letter, telegram or cable, they are said to be made by post. The rule is that an acceptance by post takes effect as soon as it is posted. If the parties have agreed to an acceptance by posting, it is complete as soon as the letter of acceptance is posted and properly addressed whether it reaches the offeror or not. If the letter is lost or delayed in the post, the contract is nevertheless made even though the offeror is ignorant of that fact.

In the case of Household Fire Insurance Co v Grant,[13] G applied for shares in a company. A letter of allotment was posted but never reached G.

Held: G was a shareholder in the company.

The postal acceptance rule is a rule of convenience laid down by the Court. This special rule of convenience only applies where the postal acceptance is prescribed by the offeror or indicated by the terms of the offer or is the common sense mode of acceptance in the circumstances. The justification for the rule is that it is easier to prove posting than it is to prove receipt of letter. The overriding consideration is reasonableness. If the offer is by post, it is reasonable to use the post for acceptance unless the offer states otherwise. If the offer is not by post it is a question of fact whether it will be reasonable to accept by post. But this special rule does not apply if the parties cannot have intended that there should be a binding agreement until the acceptance was received.

In Henthorn v Fraser,[14] F, representing a building society, offered in writing to sell certain houses to H, the offer to remain open for 14 days. H received the offer in person. Next day the following events took place:

13. (1879) 4 Ex D. 216
14. [1892] 2 Ch. 27

Midday: The society posted a letter to H revoking the offer.

3.50 pm: H posted a letter to the society accepting the offer.

5 pm: H received the society's revocation.

Held: a contract was made at 3.50 pm when H posted his letter of acceptance. Per Lord Herschell: "Where the circumstances are such that it must have been within the contemplation of the parties that, according to the ordinary usages of mankind, the post might be used as a means of communicating the acceptance of an offer, the acceptance is complete as soon as it is posted."

In Adam v Lindsell,[15] L made an offer by letter to A requiring an answer "in course of post". The letter of offer was misdirected and delayed in the post. A posted a letter of acceptance immediately. But L assumed that the absence of a reply within the expected period indicated non-acceptance and sold his goods to another buyer.

Held: the acceptance was made "in course of post" (no time limit was imposed) and effective when posted.

In Howell Securities v Hughes,[16] H granted HS an option to purchase land to be exercised "by notice in writing". A letter giving notice of the exercise of the option was lost in the post.

Held: the words "notice in writing" must mean notice received by the vendor. Therefore, notice had not been given to accept the offer (ie, the option).

A letter is posted when it is put into the official letter box or into the hands of the employee of the Post Office who is authorised to receive letters. It is not posting to put the letter into the hands of a postman who is authorised to deliver letters only.

14. Cross-offers

What is the effect of 2 offers, identical in terms, which cross in the post? Does agreement result from cross-offers?

---

15. (1818) 1 B & Ald. 681
16. [1974] 1 All E.R. 161

Suppose A by letter offers to sell his car to B for $10,000 and B, by a second letter which crosses the first letter in the post, offers to buy it for $10,000. Do these 2 letters create a contract?

The point was discussed in the case of Tinn v Hoffmann & Co[17] where it was held obiter dicta that there was no contract.

The strict requirements of offer and acceptance had not been satisfied.

15. Acceptance Subject to Contract

Acceptance "subject to contract" is not acceptance nor rejection by counter-offer. It means that the parties do not intend to be bound until a formal contract is signed by them. Unless otherwise agreed, the contract is made when a formal contract is signed by both parties.

In Chillingworth v Esche,[18] C and D signed an agreement for the purchase of a house by D "subject to a proper contract" to be prepared by C's solicitors. A contract was prepared by C's solicitors and approved by D's solicitors, but D refused to sign it.

Held: there was no contract as the agreement was only conditional.

16. The Agreement

When offer and acceptance correspond, the parties have reached an agreement. There is thus a consensus *ad idem* (agreement on the same points). A valid contract has come into existence provided the other requirements such as consideration and intention to create legal relations, etc, are met.

---

17. (1873) 29 L.T. 271
18. [1924] 1 Ch. 97

3 Intention to Create Legal Relations

Intention to create legal relations is an element necessary for the formation of a contract. An agreement is not a binding contract unless the parties intend to create legal relations. In other words, an agreement is not a contract if the parties did not intend that it should be legally binding or that it should have legal consequences. Intention to create legal relations means the readiness of each party to accept the legal consequences if he does not perform his contract.

If parties indicate that they do not wish their agreement to be binding on them, the law would respect their intention.

In Rose and Frank v J.R. Crompton & Bros,[1] a commercial agreement by which A (a British manufacturer) appointed B to be its distributor in the USA expressly stated that it was "not subject to legal jurisdiction" in either country. A terminated the agreement without giving notice as was required and refused to deliver goods ordered by B although A had accepted these orders when placed. Held: the general agreement was not legally binding but the orders for goods were separate and binding contracts.

It is convenient here to classify contracts under domestic and social agreements, and commercial agreements.

1. Domestic and Social Agreements

In the case of domestic and social agreements there is a presumption that there is no intention to create legal relations because the agreements are based on mutual trust and affection. For example, your friend promises to go for a walk with you and he does not do so. Can you sue him? The answer is "No".

---

1. [1923] 2 K.B. 261

Similarly, domestic agreements such as a husband agreeing to give his wife pocket money are not contractually binding.

In Balfour v Balfour,[2] the husband was employed in Ceylon. He and his wife returned to the UK on leave but it was agreed that for health reasons she would not return to Ceylon with him. He promised to pay £30 per month as maintenance. He did not keep the promise and the wife sued him.

Held: This was an informal agreement made between husband and wife and was not intended to be legally binding.

In Jones v Padavatton,[3] a mother wanted her daughter to study law in England. At a time when mother and daughter were very close, the mother bought a house in London to enable the daughter to reside there during her studies. Later, differences arose and the mother claimed possession of the house.

Held: the arrangement in relation to the house was not intended to be legally binding and that the mother was entitled to possession of the house.

The presumption that there is no intention to create legal relations in domestic and social agreements may be rebutted. Thus, even if the parties are in a domestic or social relationship but intend their agreement to have legal consequences, an enforceable contract is concluded.

In Merritt v Merritt,[4] the husband had left the matrimonial home, which was owned by him, to live with another woman. Husband and wife met and held a discussion in the husband's car in the course of which he agreed to pay her £40 per month out of which she agreed to keep up the mortgage payments on the house. The wife refused to leave the car until the husband signed a note of these agreed terms and an undertaking to transfer the house to her sole name when the mortgage had been paid off. The wife paid off the mortgage but the husband refused to transfer the house to her.

Held: in the circumstances intention to create legal relations was to be inferred and the wife could sue for breach of contract. The rule in the Balfour case did not apply to husband

2. [1919] 2 K.B. 571
3. [1979] 2 All E.R. 166
4. [1970] 1 W.L.R. 1211

and wife who are not living in amity. In the present case husband and wife negotiated at arm's length as they had decided to separate and reasonable persons would regard their agreement as intended to be binding in law. The wife was entitled to sue.

In Simpkins v Pays,[5] a widow, her grandmother and a paying lodger agreed to take part together each week in a newspaper competition. The entries were made in the defendant's (grand-mother's) name but there was no rule as to the payment of postage expenses. One week the entry was successful and the defendant obtained the prize money. The plaintiff (lodger) claimed a third of the prize money. But the defendant refused to pay on the ground that there was no intention to create legal relations but only a friendly adventure.

Held: the plaintiff won the case. On the present facts, it was a joint enterprise to which each contributed in the expectation of sharing any prize that was won. In other words, the parties intended to create legal relations, ie, to form an informal syndicate and that the recipient of the prize money had to share it with the others.

2. Commercial Agreements

In commercial agreements there is a rebuttable presumption that the parties do intend to make a legally enforceable contract.

Sometimes parties may agree that their agreement, although couched in legal terms, shall not be binding in law but shall be binding "in honour" only. Agreements binding "in honour" only would not be a contract. If the parties expressly declare that the transaction is not to be binding in law, the Court will give effect to that declaration.

In Rose & Frank Co v Crompton Bros Ltd,[6] Company R made an agreement with Company C whereby Company R was appointed the agent for the sale of paper supplied by the Company C. A clause in the agreement was: "This arrangement is not entered into as a formal or legal agreement and shall not be subject to legal jurisdiction in the law courts."

---

5. [1955] 1 W.L.R. 975
6. supra.

Held: no contract was made between the parties and that the agreement could not be sued upon.

Similarly, if a company assumes a moral but not legal obligation to help another, then the agreement will be deemed to have no contractual effect. "Comfort Letters", for example, in which one company assures another that the business of a third will meet its liabilities in line with its policy will not have any contractual effect

Kleinwort Benson Ltd v Malaysia Mining Corp. Bhd[7]

> The plaintiff bank agreed with the Defendant to make a loan facility of up to £10 million available to the defendant's wholly owned subsidiary M which traded in tin on the London Metal Exchange. As part of the arrangement the defendant furnished to the plaintiff two letters of comfort each which stated that "it is our policy to ensure that the business of [M] is at all times in a position to meet its liabilities to you under the [loan facility] agreements." In 1985, the tin market collapsed and M went into liquidation owing the plaintiffs the whole loan. The plaintiff sought payment from the defendant who refused to pay. The plaintiff brought an action against them, and the judge held that the plaintiff was entitled to recover. The defendant appealed.
>
> *Held:* A letter of comfort from a parent company to a lender did not have contractual effect if it was merely a statement of fact regarding the parent company's intention and was not a contractual promise as to the parent company's future conduct. On the facts, the letters of comfort were in terms a statement of present fact and not a promise as to future conduct and in the context in which the letters were written was not intended to be anything other than a representation of fact giving rise to no more than a moral responsibility on the part of the defendant's to meet M's debt. Appeal allowed.

---

7. [1989] 1 All E.R. 785

4 Consideration

1. What is Consideration?
Consideration was defined in Curries v Misa[1] as
> "some right, interest, profit or benefit accruing to one party, or some forbearance, detriment, loss or responsibility given, suffered or undertaken by the other".

Consideration is some benefit received by a party who gives a promise or performs an act or some detriment suffered by a party who receives a promise. The benefit accruing or the detriment sustained is in return for a promise given or received.

Illustrations
(a) X receives $100 in return for which he promises to deliver goods to B. The consideration is the money X receives for the promise he makes to deliver the goods.
(b) E promises to deliver goods to F, and F promises to pay for the goods on delivery. The benefit E receives is F's promise to pay, and in return for it he promises to deliver the goods.

2. Types of Consideration
There are 3 types of consideration:
   (a) Past consideration;
   (b) Executed consideration; and
   (c) Executory consideration.

(a) *Past Consideration*
Consideration is past if a promise is made in return for an act that has already been performed. A past consideration is not a

---
1. (1875) L.R. 10 Ex 153

good consideration in law. Suppose Y sues to enforce a promise and the only consideration he gives is a past consideration, he will fail in his action.

Illustration

X promises Y $10 because Y dug K's garden last Monday.

Y cannot sue on that promise because the consideration furnished by Y is a past consideration. When K's promise was made Y's act was already in the past.

(b) Executed Consideration

An executed consideration is an act done by one party in exchange for a promise made or an act done by the other. When the act constituting the consideration is completely performed the consideration is said to be executed.

Illustration

E offers a reward for the return of his lost dog, and F finds and returns the dog to E and claims the reward. F has already performed his consideration when he makes the claim. That is executed consideration and valid. (When F made his claim, his act was in the past, but his act did not occur before E made his promise).

(c) Executory Consideration

An executory consideration is a promise made by one party in exchange for a promise made or an act done by the other. Where the consideration is a promise to be performed in the future, it is executory. A promise is an executory consideration that something will be done in the future. An executory consideration is perfectly valid.

Illustration

S promises to deliver goods to B. B promises to pay for the goods when delivered. The benefit S receives is B's promise to pay and in return for it he promises to deliver the goods.

3. Rules on Consideration

The following are some rules governing consideration:

(a) Consideration required for all Simple Contracts

Consideration is an essential element in every simple contract, ie, contract not under seal. The doctrine of consideration is that an agreement will only be enforceable as a contract if it contains consideration, ie, it will only be binding as a contract if it is a bargain. A promise without consideration is a gift; one made for consideration is a bargain.

(b) Consideration must be Sufficient or Real but need not be Adequate

Sufficient consideration means such consideration as the law will recognise. For example, past consideration is not sufficient consideration. Consideration need not be adequate to the promise but must be of some value. As long as some value has been given, the Court will not ask whether adequate value has been given. It is a matter for the parties themselves to determine what they consider is the proper value of their promise. It is not part of the court's duty to assess the relative value of each party's contribution to the bargain. But inadequacy of consideration may be evidence of fraud. If the agreement is freely reached, the inadequacy of the price is immaterial to the existence of a binding contract.

Illustration

> X promises to sell his BMW car to Y for $20. X now refuses to sell for that price. Y sues X. In the absence of fraud, X had just made a bad bargain and Y is entitled to buy the car for $20. Here money is sufficient consideration but the value need not be adequate.

In Chappell & Co Ltd v Nestle Co Ltd,[2] the Nestle Co offered to the public gramophone records of a certain dance tune for 1s 6d each together with 3 choc bar wrappers. The wrappers were thrown away on receipt by the company. On the question whether the wrappers were part of the

---

2. [1960] A.C. 87

consideration given for each record, it was held that the wrappers were part of the consideration even though they were of no further value once received by the company.

(c) Consideration must be Legal
An illegal consideration makes the whole contract invalid.

(d) Consideration must not be Past
Consideration which is past is not sufficient consideration. A past consideration is one which is wholly finished before the promise is made.

Suppose X offers to drive Y from Singapore to Kuala Lumpur in his car. On arrival in Kuala Lumpur, Y promises to pay X $30 towards the cost of the petrol. Y's promise is not binding because the "consideration" for which it was given was past.

In the case of Roscorla v Thomas,[3] at T's request, R bought T's horse for 30. After the sale, T promised R that the horse was sound and free from vice. The horse proved to be vicious.

Held: there was no consideration to support T's promise and he was not bound. The sale itself could not be valuable consideration, for it was completed at the time the promise was given.

(e) Consideration must Move from the Promisee/Plaintiff
The person to whom the promise is made must furnish the consideration. Consideration which does not move from the promisee/plaintiff is not sufficient consideration. In other words, a plaintiff suing to enforce a promise will fail in his action if consideration did not move from him, as distinct from some third party. A contract is a bargain. If a person gives no consideration for a promise he cannot sue on that promise whether or not he is the person to whom the promise is made. But while consideration must move from the promisee, it need not move to the promisor.

Suppose there is an agreement between X and A that each pays money to B. X pays up. A does not. X can sue A. It does not matter that the consideration moving from X does not move to A; it is a detriment to X incurred at the request of A.

3. [1842] 3 Q.S. 234

Consideration

(f) Consideration must not be for something which the Promisor is already bound to do

If X promises to do something which he is already under a duty to do, can the promise constitute a valid consideration? No. Here X's promise is not a valid consideration. X does not contribute anything to the new bargain.

In Stilk v Myrick,[4] S, a seaman, agreed to sail on a certain voyage. Two seamen deserted the crew. The captain promised the rest of the crew that if they worked the ship back to port they would share the wages of the 2 deserters among themselves. S sued for his share. It was held that the captain's promise could not be enforced. S failed because he was already bound by contract to work the ship back. In performing their existing contractual duties the crew gave no consideration for the promise of extra pay and the promise was therefore not binding. However, where desertions had reduced the crew below the workable minimum, the crew may be held to have provided consideration by doing more than their contractual duties.

Similarly, performance of an existing obligation imposed by law, eg, to appear as a witness when called upon in a lawsuit, is no consideration for a promise of reward. But if some extra service is given that is sufficient consideration.

In Glasbrook Bros v Glamorgan County Council,[5] the fact were as follows:

> At a time of industrial unrest colliery owners asked for and agreed to pay for a special police guard on the mine. Later they repudiated liability saying that the police had done no more than perform their public duty of maintaining order.
>
> *Held:* the police had done more than perform their general duties. The extra services given were consideration for the promise to pay.

(g) Rule in Pinnel's Case — Part Payment of a Debt is no Consideration for Discharge of the Whole Debt

Payment of a smaller sum of money is not a satisfaction of an agreement to pay a larger sum even though the creditor agrees

---

4. (1809) 2 Camp. 317
5. [1925] A.C. 270

Contract Law

to take it in full discharge. This is the rule in Pinnel's case payment of a smaller sum does not discharge a larger debt.

Illustration

Suppose X owes Y $1,000. Y agrees to take $800 in full discharge. There is no consideration for the forgiveness of $200. X has not given consideration for Y's promise. So Y is not bound by his promise. X has not given consideration because he has paid only a part of what he is already contractually bound to Y to pay.

Payment on the day that a debt is due of less than the full amount of the debt is no consideration for a promise to release the balance. A debt can only be discharged by "accord and satisfaction". "Accord" is the agreement and "satisfaction" is consideration.

In the famous case of Foakes v Beer,[6] Mrs Beer obtained a judgment against Dr Foakes for £2,090. Dr Foakes asked for time to pay and the parties agreed that Mrs Beer would not "take any proceedings whatsoever on the judgement" if Dr Foakes paid that amount in stated instalments. After Dr Foakes had paid off the debt, Mrs Beer sued him for interest on the debt. It was held that Mrs Beer was entitled to recover interest as there was no real consideration for the agreement to pay by instalments.

Qualifications to the Rule in Pinnel's Case

The following are important qualifications[7] to the rule in Pinnel's case:

(a) Payment of a smaller sum before due day at the creditor's request is valid consideration.

(b) Payment of a smaller sum, at a different place, at the creditor's request is valid consideration.

(c) Payment of a smaller sum accompanied, at the creditor's request, by delivery of a chattel is valid. For example, the gift of a pen or pencil, etc, in satisfaction is good.

---

6. (1884) 9 App. Cas. 605
7. Payment of a smaller sum by cheque is no discharge of the balance. See D. and C. Suilders Ltd v Sees [1966] 2 Q.S. 617.

(d) Payment of part of a debt is made by a third party. If such payment is accepted by the creditor in full settlement, the payment is a good defence to a later action by the creditor against the debtor for the balance.[8]

Suppose X owes Y $200 and Z promises Y $150 on condition that Y will discharge X. If the $150 is paid and Y still sues X for the balance, Y will fail in his action. To allow the claim would be a fraud on Z.

(e) A composition agreement is an agreement between a debtor and all his creditors that he will pay them and that they will accept a dividend in full settlement of their claims. A creditor who has received a dividend under such an agreement will fail if he sues the debtor for the balance of his original claim. This qualification is also based on the idea of fraud and to allow the creditor to claim would be a fraud on the other creditors.

4. Promissory Estoppel

The doctrine of promissory estoppel may prevent a person from retracting his promise. Equity does not look with favour on a man who promises relief to another and then goes back on his promise. An agreement, though without consideration, will create legal relations if acted on by the promisee, and will be binding, on the promisor and he will not be allowed to act inconsistently with it. This principle is called promissory estoppel. This doctrine of promissory estoppel applies only where it is inequitable for the promisor to go back on his promise.

Illustration

Suppose Y (creditor) makes a promise (unsupported by consideration) to X (debtor) that Y will not insist on the full discharge of the debt and the promise is made with the intention that X should act on it and he does so. Y is estopped (prohibited) from retracting his promise unless X can be restored to his original position. Y will be prevented from retracting his

---

8. Hirachand Punamchand v Temple [1911] 2 K.B. 330

promise with retrospective effect though it may permit him to insist on his full rights in the future.

In the famous case of Central London Property Trust Ltd v High Trees House Ltd,[9] the facts were as follows:

> In 1939 Y let a block of flats to X at an annual rent of £2,500 p.a. It was difficult to let the individual flats in wartime. Y agreed in writing to accept a reduced rent of £1,250 p.a. No time limit was set on the arrangement but it was related to wartime conditions. The reduced rent was paid from 1940 to 1945 and X let flats during the period on the basis of its expected liability to pay rent under the head lease at £1,250 p.a. only. In 1945 the flats were fully let. Y demanded a full rent of £2,500 p.a. for (i) part of the previous period in which £1,250 p.a. had been accepted; and (ii) for the future.
>
> *Held:* Y was entitled to the full rent of £2,500 p.a. for the future only, ie, claim (ii) was valid but claim (i) was rejected on the grounds of promissory estoppel.

Promissory estoppel applies only to a waiver of existing rights. A promise which creates new obligations is not binding unless supported by consideration. The doctrine of promissory estoppel is "a shield and not a sword". It can be used as a defence but not a cause of action.

In the case of Combe v Combe,[10] the facts were as follows:

> A wife obtained a divorce decree nisi against her husband. He then promised her that he would make maintenance payments. The wife did not apply to the Court for an order for maintenance but this forbearance was not at the husband's request. The decree was made absolute. The husband paid no maintenance. The wife sued him on his promise. In the High Court the wife obtained judgment on the basis of promissory estoppel. On appeal, it was held that promissory estoppel does not create new causes of action where none existed before. It only prevents a party from insisting on his strict legal rights when it would be unjust to allow him to enforce them. The wife's claim therefore failed.

9. [1947] K.B. 130
10. [1951] 2 K.B. 215

5 Form of Contract

As a general rule, a contract may be made in any form, ie, in writing or by word of mouth or implication by conduct. For example, a customer in a self-service shop takes his selected goods to the cash desk, pays for them. There is a contract of sale although not a word has been spoken.

The formal requirements of a contract can be discussed under 3 headings:
— contracts under seal or by deed;
— contracts which must be in writing; and
— contracts which must be evidenced in writing.

1. Contracts under Seal or by Deed

A contract under seal (also known as a deed or specialty contract) is a contract which is in writing and is signed, sealed and delivered. A deed takes effect from the date when it is delivered.

No consideration is required for contracts under seal. In contrast, simple contracts require consideration. Contracts made without consideration such as a deed of gift must be under seal.

2. Contracts which must be in Writing

Some types of contract are required to be in the form of a written document and are void (ie, destitute of all legal effect) if not in that form. The following contracts are valid only if in writing:
— contracts of marine insurance;
— bills of exchange and promissory notes;

Contract Law

— hire-purchase agreements;
— transfer of shares of a registered company;
— mortgage and transfer of ships; and
— mortgages, charges and leases exceeding 3 years under the Singapore Land Titles Act.

3. Contracts which must be Evidenced in Writing

Certain types of contract are enforceable only if they can be proved by written evidence. The contracts under this category are:

    (i) contracts relating to land;[1] and
    (ii) contracts of guarantee.[2]

An unenforceable contract is one which is valid but it cannot be enforced by action because of some technical defect such as the absence of a note or memorandum in writing required by the Statute of Frauds 1677 (UK).

The agreement itself need not be in writing. It is sufficient if there is a signed note or memorandum in writing. The note must contain:

— the names of the parties;
— all the material terms; and
— a description of the subject-matter.

The note must be signed by the party to be charged. In other words, it is only the party against whom the contract is being enforced who need sign.

The written evidence need not be provided in a single document but if it is contained in more than one document there must be an express or implicit reference in one document to another.

In Pearce v Gardner,[3] a letter written by the defendant to the plaintiff began "Dear Sir". It did not identify the addressee. But it was complete evidence of all the other required matters. The plaintiff produced the envelope, addressed to him by name, in which the letter had been sent.

Held: the letter implied that it had been posted in an

---

1. See Section 53 of the Conveyancing and Law of Property Act (Cap. 268)
2. Section 4 of the Statute of Frauds 1677 (UK)
3. [1897] 1 Q.B. 688

envelope and the plaintiff might give oral evidence to produce and identify the envelope as the one in which the letter had been received.

Where there is no sufficient written evidence the contract is unenforceable, but it is not a void contract.

4. Doctrine of Part Performance

If there is no memorandum (or sufficient written evidence) the contract cannot be enforced except in certain cases where there has been part performance. This exception relates almost entirely to contracts for the sale of land. The requirement of written evidence can produce a very unfair result for a party to an oral contract for the sale of land who incurs expense in performing his obligations and then finds that the other party refuses to perform his. Equity offers relief from that hardship by treating performance of the contract as evidence of the contract. Although unenforceable at law, a contract relating to land is enforceable in equity — doctrine of part performance.

The effect of this doctrine is that a party who has partly performed a contract may obtain specific performance[4] even though there is no written evidence of the contract. The act of part performance must be such as to point clearly to some contract and must at least be consistent with the particular contract that is alleged.

Payment of money is not by itself a sufficient act of part performance because it might have all manner of explanations. The mere payment of money is equivocal. But that does not mean that payment of money could never be a sufficient act of part performance.[5] As Cheshire and Fifoot put it, "... Probably the payment of money will continue to be regarded as usually equivocal but as capable of being rendered persuasive by the surrounding circumstances."

Entry into possession of the land in question is a very strong act of part performance because it is hardly explicable except on the basis of the alleged contract.

The doctrine of part performance was applied in the following 2 cases:

---

4. The equitable remedy of specific performance is explained in Chapter 14
5. Steadman v Steadman [1974] Q.B. 161

Contract Law

Maddison v Alderson[6]

M lived for some years with A as his housekeeper. He failed to pay her wages and she planned to leave and get married. A then promised M orally that if she would continue as his housekeeper without wages until his death A would leave her a life interest in his farm under his will. She continued on this basis as A's housekeeper until A died. A's will gave effect to his promise but it was unattested and so void as a will. M claimed against A's executor alleging part performance of an oral contract by which her unpaid services were the price by which she purchased her life interest.

Held: M's claim must fail since M's conduct was not "unequivocally referable" to the alleged contract. She might have continued as A's housekeeper for some other reason.

However, in modern cases the Court has adopted a less demanding test, ie, an act of part performance is sufficient if it indicates that there is some contract between the parties and is not inconsistent with the particular contract alleged by the plaintiff. It need no longer be the only possible explanation; it suffices if it is one possible explanation.

Wakeham v Mackenzie[7]

A lost his wife when he was 70. Two years later he agreed orally with B, a widow of 67, that if she would move from her council flat into his house and look after him until he died he would leave her his house and its contents at his death. While living with him B was to pay for her board and fuel. B carried out her part of the contract but A did not leave the house and its contents to her by his will.

Held: B's conduct was sufficient part performance of the contract. Unlike the case of Maddison v Alderson, B had moved from her flat to A's house and she had paid a contribution to the household expenses. These acts pointed strongly enough to the existence of a bargain such as B alleged had been made. Specific performance in favour of B was ordered against A's executor.

---

6. (1883) 8 App. Cas. 467
7. [1969] 2 All E.R. 783

5. No Formalities Required

Where no form is required, then a contract can be in any form. It can thus be made orally. Most contracts in daily life including business deals are contracted orally. The difference between an oral contract and a written one is the question of proof. So long as the party suing on an oral contract can prove its existence, it will be enforced by the Court.

6 Capacity

Generally, all persons have full legal power to enter into any contract and bind themselves. But a few categories of persons do not have this power in full. They are said to be under incapacity. These persons are minors, corporations, mentally disordered persons and drunkards.

1. Minors

Incapacity is imposed by law upon a minor, not as a punishment, but to protect him from the consequences of his inexperience. A minor is a person below the age of 21 years old.[1]

Minors' contracts are divided into 3 groups:
 (a) valid contracts;
 (b) voidable contracts; and
 (c) void contracts.

(a) Valid Contracts

These are contracts for necessaries and education for the minor's benefit. A minor is bound by such contracts.

(i) Necessaries

The term "necessaries" has been held to include goods and services necessary to the minor according to his station in life.

---

1. In Singapore, the English law on the age of majority will apply. The problem of applying English law is that the Family Law Reform Act 1969 (UK) lowered the age of majority from 21 to 18 years. Under Section 5(1) of the Civil Law Act (Cap. 30), English law is applicable to mercantile law generally if questions or issues arise with respect to such a law. If the English statute on capacity is applicable, then the age of majority in Singapore for the purpose of contract would also be lowered from 21 to 18 years. But the Family Law Reform Act (UK) is not really a law dealing with "mercantile" matters but with the law of status. Thus there is uncertainty as to the age of majority in mercantile matters.

For example, a watch and a radio may be considered to be necessaries but not luxury articles. The Court elaborated on the nature of necessaries in the case of Chapple v Cooper:[2]

> "... the subject matter and extent of the contract may vary according to the state and condition of the infant himself. His clothes may be fine or coarse according to his rank; his education may vary according to the station he is to fill; and the medicines may depend on the illness with which he is afflicted, and the extent of his probable means when of age. But in all these cases, it must first be made out that the class itself is one in which the things furnished are essential to the existence and reasonable advantage and comfort of the infant contractor. Thus articles of mere luxury are always excluded."

When the necessaries are goods, the minor is only liable when goods are:
— suitable to his condition in life;
— necessary to his requirements at the time of sale;
— necessary to his requirements at the time of delivery; and
— goods with which he was not sufficiently supplied at the time of sale and delivery.

Therefore necessaries would normally include food, medicine and clothes for the minor and his dependants, if any.

A minor need only pay a reasonable price for necessaries supplied to him. The minor must actually need the goods supplied. Although the goods supplied may be necessary, they may not be necessary to the particular minor if a minor is already amply supplied with the goods as illustrated in Nash v Inman.[3] The facts were as follows:

> A minor was an undergrad at Cambridge. He bought 11 fancy waistcoats from N, the tailor. He was at the time of purchase adequately provided with clothes.
> *Held:* the waistcoats were not necessary and the minor was not liable to pay for any of them.

---

2. (1844) 13 M. & W. 252
3. [1908] 2 K.B. 1

(ii) Educational Contracts

Education has been held to be necessary. This includes contracts under which a minor obtains education, training for a trade or beneficial apprenticeship in a profession. For example, in Roberts v Gray,[4] a contract which helped a minor to learn billiards so that he may become a professional player was considered as a contract for necessaries.

Under the Sale of Goods Act 1979, the capacity to buy and sell goods is regulated by the general law relating to contractual capacity. Section 3 of the Sale of Goods Act defines necessaries as "goods suitable to the condition in life of the minor or other person concerned and to his actual requirements at the time of the sale and delivery."

(b) Voidable Contracts

A voidable contract is a contract which a minor may avoid, ie, terminate at his options. It is voidable in the sense that it is binding on the minor unless he repudiates it before he reaches majority or within a reasonable time after majority. The other party cannot repudiate. Contracts that are voidable at the option of the minor include tenancy agreements, partnership agreements and agreements to purchase shares not fully paid up. For example, if a minor rents a flat, he will have to pay rent for the period leased unless he repudiates the contract within a reasonable time after attaining majority.

(c) Void Contracts

The following contracts by a minor are absolutely void:
  (i) for the repayment of money lent or to be lent;
  (ii) for goods supplied or to be supplied (other than necessaries); and
  (iii) all accounts stated with minors.

A void contract is no contract at all. A minor cannot ratify the above void contracts after attaining majority. But a minor may make an entirely fresh contract after full age.

The "money lent or to be lent" means lent or to be lent to a minor. The "goods supplied or to be supplied" means goods supplied or to be supplied to a minor. An "account stated" means an acknowledgement of a debt.

---

4. [1913] 1 K.B. 520

Capacity

Coutts & Co v Browne-Lecky[5]

B, a minor, had an overdraft with the bank. X and Y guaranteed it. The bank sued X and Y for payment. *Held:* as the loan by the bank to B was void (ie, no contract at all) X and Y could not be liable.

Even if the minor fraudulently states that he is of full age so as to induce the other party to give him credit, the contract is void. When a contract is void, it is treated as if it had never existed. The injured party cannot sue for fraud. To allow him to do so would be giving him an indirect means of enforcing the void contract.

Leslie v Sheill[6]

S, a minor, by fraudulently representing himself to be of full age induced L to lend him £400. S refused to repay the loan and L sued him. S pleaded minority as a defence. *Held:* the Infants Relief Act 1874 made the contract void. S was not liable to repay the £400. L could not recover the loan even under fraud because, if allowed, it would be an indirect way of enforcing this void contract.

2. Corporations

A corporation or a company is an artificial legal person. It is distinct from the individual persons who are shareholders of the corporation. It has a legal existence separate and distinct from the shareholders.

The powers of a corporation, set up under the Companies Act (Cap 185), are limited by the objects set out in the memorandum of association. Thus, a company can only contract within the objects set out in the memorandum of association. Any activity outside the objects clause in the memorandum of association is *ultra vires* (ie, beyond the powers) and void.

Salomon v Salomon & Co Ltd[7]

Salomon, a boot manufacturer, was the owner of a profitable business. At a time when he and his business

---

5. [1947] K.B. 104
6. [1914] 3 K.B. 607
7. [1897] A.C. 22

were perfectly solvent, he converted his business into a company limited by shares. He took 20,000 shares and his wife and 5 children took one share each (at that time the minimum number of shareholders in all companies was 7). No other shares were issued. Salomon also received a debenture to the amount of 10,000 which was secured by a charge on all the assets of the company. Later the company became insolvent.
Held: the debenture took priority over the unsecured creditors. The "one man company" was a person different in law from the controlling shareholder.

3. Mentally Disordered and Drunken Persons

If a person, at the time of contracting, is suffering from a mental disability and is incapable of understanding the nature of the contract, the contract is voidable at his instance if he can prove that his disability was known to the other party.

Imperial Loan Co v Stone[8]
> L sued S on a promissory note. S pleaded that he was insane at the time he made it.
> *Held:* for S to succeed he must prove he was insane at the material time and that L knew of his insanity.

In the case of a drunken person, a contract is voidable by the drunken party only if he could not understand the transaction and the other party knows about his condition. A contract made by a man when drunk can be ratified when he is sober.

Both mentally disordered and drunken persons are liable for necessaries supplied to them while suffering from such incapacity. In such a case they are bound to pay a reasonable price for the necessaries.[9]

4. Minors Contracts Act

By the Minors Contracts Act 1987, a court can, if it seems just and equitable, require an infant to transfer to the other person any property obtained by the infant under the contract. So a court may now order the return of the waistcoats.

S 3 MCA 1987

---

8. [1892] 1 Q.B. 599
9. Section 3 of the Sale of Goods Act 1979 (UK)

7 Terms of Contract

1. Terms and Representations
The "terms of a contract" must be distinguished from "mere representations". In practice, many contracts are entered into after negotiations. Representations are statements of fact made by one party to the other in the course of negotiations with a view to inducing the other to enter into a contract. Representations are made before a contract is concluded. If the mere representation is false then it is a misrepresentation. It is possible that a representation may become embodied in a contract and then it becomes a term of the contract.

Suppose B wishes to buy S's car. In the course of negotiations, S may tell B that his car goes 50 km per litre. Because of this statement B buys the car. Later B finds that the car goes only 30 km per litre. The first issue to decide is whether there has been a representation or whether there has been a breach of any contractual term. The statement (50 km per litre) made by S, which is a representation, may have become embodied in the contract and become a term of the contract.

If it is a mere representation, then the usual law relating to misrepresentation will apply (see Chapter 9). But if it has become a term of the contract then there will be a breach of a contractual term.

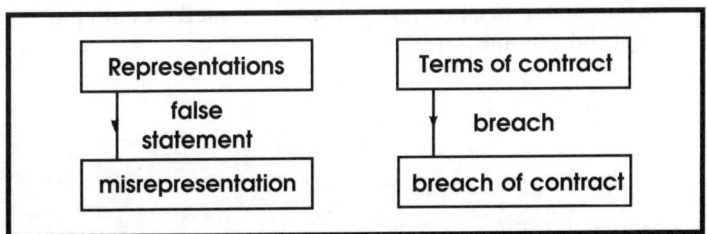

2. Terms of a Contract

The terms of a contract set out the rights and obligations of the parties. Contractual terms may be express or implied.

3. Express Terms

Express terms are terms which the contracting parties state expressly either orally or in writing or partly orally and partly in writing.

Where a contract is made wholly orally, its terms are a matter of evidence from the words the parties used.

Parol Evidence Rule

Where a contract is wholly in writing the general rule is that parol evidence cannot be admitted to add to, vary or contradict a written document. "Parol" means any extrinsic (outside) evidence. Once the parties have reduced their agreement to writing, they are confined to the four corners of the documents and are therefore bound by the writing alone. Therefore, evidence of the parties' negotiations before the contract is excluded. Similarly, evidence of the parties' post-contractual behaviour is not admissible to show their intentions.

Limits to the Parol Evidence Rule

(a) Extrinsic evidence is admissible to show that the contract does not yet operate.
In Pym v Campbell,[1] a written agreement for the sale of a patent was drawn up and evidence was admitted of an oral stipulation that the agreement should not become operative until a third party approved of the invention.
(b) Evidence may be admitted to prove a custom or trade usage thereby adding terms which do not appear on the face of the document.
(c) Evidence may be admitted to rectify a written document where it can be shown that it was executed by both parties under a common mistake.

---

1. (1856) 6 E. & S. 370

4. Implied Terms

Implied terms are those terms which are not expressly stated but are implied in law. A term will be implied if it is necessary to carry out the presumed intention of the parties, ie, if it is necessary to give business efficacy to the contract which the parties intended. Such terms are so obvious that the parties must have intended them to apply to the contract and therefore thought that it was unnecessary to express them.

The leading case is the Moorcock case.[2] The facts were as follows:

> The owners of a wharf agreed that a ship should be moored alongside to unload its cargo. It was known to both wharfingers and shipowners that at low tide the ship would ground on the mud at the bottom. At ebb tide the ship struck a ridge of rock and was damaged.
> *Held:* it was an implied term that the ground alongside the wharf was safe at low tide. Therefore the wharfingers were liable for damages as they were in breach of the implied term.

Custom, however, may not be implied to contradict an express term in a contract. This is illustrated by the case of Les Affreteurs Reunis Societe Anonyme v Walford:[3]

> A charter of a ship provided expressly for a commission to be paid on signing the charter. There was a trade custom that it should be paid only when hire had actually been earned.
> *Held:* Custom should only be given effect to where it is consistent with the plain words of a contract.

Certain terms are implied by statute although the parties have not specifically agreed on them. For example, in the sale of goods a seller of goods impliedly undertakes that the goods sold are fit for the purpose for which the buyer requires them or that they are of merchantable quality.

---

2. (1889) 14 P.D. 64
3. [1919] A.C. 801

5. Conditions and Warranties

The terms of a contract may be classified by their relative importance as:
- conditions; and
- warranties.

A condition is a vital term of a contract going to the root of the contract. A breach of condition entitles the injuredparty to repudiate the contract (ie, treat the contract as discharged) and to claim damages.

A warranty is not a vital term in a contract but is merely subsidiary to the contract. A breach of warranty merely gives rise to an action for damages and does not entitle the injured party to repudiate the contract.

Since there is a stronger remedy available for breach of condition than for breach of warranty it is usual for the parties to be in dispute as to whether a term is a condition or a warranty. The difference is illustrated by 2 cases:

Poussard v Spiers[4]

> Poussard agreed to sing in an opera throughout a series of performances. Owing to illness she was unable to appear on the opening night and the next few days. The producer engaged a substitute. When Poussard had recovered the producer declined to accept her services for the remaining performances.
> *Held:* the failure to sing on the opening night was a breach of condition which entitled the producer to treat the contract for the remaining performances as discharged.

Bettini v Gye[5]

> An opera singer was engaged for a series of performances under a contract which required him to be in London for rehearsals 6 days before the opening performance. Owing to illness he did not arrive until the third day before the opening. The producer sought on this ground to terminate the contract.

4. (1876) 1 Q.B.D. 410
5. (1876) 1 Q.B.D. 183

Held: the rehearsal clause was subsidiary to the main purpose of the contract. Breach of the clause must be treated as a breach of warranty. Therefore the producer was bound to accept the singer's services and he could only claim for damages.

Whether a term in a contract is a warranty or a condition would depend on the intention of the parties which is to be deduced from the circumstances of the case. The use by the parties of the terms "conditions" and "warranties" is not conclusive of their meaning. In other words, where the parties describe a term as a condition it is still open to the Court to hold that the term is a warranty.[6]

6. Complex Terms

The traditional distinction between conditions and warranties is no longer regarded as exhaustive because it takes no account of stipulations which are neither conditions nor warranties. Such stipulations; known as complex terms, are of a different character and their effect depends on the consequences of breach.

Such complex terms combine the nature of a condition and a warranty in so far as in some events the breach of such undertakings may entitle the innocent party to repudiate and in other events, the breach may entitle him only to claim damages but not to repudiate the contract.

An example of a complex term is: "A shipowner undertakes in a charter party to provide a seaworthy ship." Such an undertaking can be broken by the presence of trivial defects easily and rapidly remediable, or such an undertaking can also be broken by serious defects going to the root of the contract and thus entitling the injured party to repudiate the contract.

---

6. Schuler A.G. v Wickman Machine Tool Sales [1974] A.C. 235

8 Exemption Clauses

An exemption clause is a contractual stipulation purporting to limit or exclude the liability of one of the parties. A common example of an exemption clause is found in parking areas where the owners of car parks put up notices to the effect that they "will not be responsible for any damage, loss or injury" to cars parked on the premises.

Exemption clauses found in standard form contracts are:
  (a) Charterparty, bill of lading and insurance policies. Terms are negotiated between persons of equal bargaining strength. Therefore strong presumption that terms are fair and reasonable.
  (b) The same presumption does not apply to other kinds of standard form contract where there is inequality of bargaining power, for example, the take-it-or-leave-it kind such as air-tickets.

It follows from the doctrine of freedom of contract that parties are free to include in contracts exemption clauses such as the above warning to car owners. If a car is stolen, can the owner of the car park rely on an exemption clause?

There are restrictions on this freedom to use exemption clauses. They cannot be against public policy. They cannot be imposed where statute prohibits or restricts it. The Court does not favour exemption clauses in contracts and both statutory and judicial restrictions have been imposed on their employment. The general effect of the Common Law and statutory rules is to narrow the scope of exemption clauses. But they still continue to be important in contracts between traders (where the parties should be able to negotiate on the basis of equal knowledge of the law).

Exemption Clauses

1. Judicial Restrictions

For many years, the Court developed various rules of case law to restrain the effectiveness of exemption clauses.

(a) To be effective, an exemption clause must be in a contractual document and not in a mere receipt. In other words, the exemption clause must be put forward in a document which gives reasonable notice that liability conditions are proposed by it.

Chapelton v Barry UDC[1]
There was a pile of deck chairs and a notice stating: "Hire of chairs 2d per session of 3 hours." The plaintiff took 2 chairs, paid for them and received 2 tickets which he put in his pocket. One of the chairs collapsed and he was injured. The defendant Council relied on a notice on the back of the tickets to disclaim liability.
Held: the notice advertising chairs for hire gave no warning of limiting conditions and it was not reasonable to communicate them on a receipt. The exemption clause did not protect the Council because the ticket was a mere receipt.

(b) If a person signs a contractual document, he is bound by its terms including any exemption clause it may contain, even if he does not read the document.

L'Estrange v Graucob[2]
A sold to B, a shopkeeper, a slot machine under conditions which excluded B's normal rights under the Sale of Goods Act. B signed the document without reading the relevant condition. The machine did not work properly.
Held: A was protected by the exemption clause which was binding on B who had signed the contract.

(c) Where a person can prove that he was induced to sign a contractual document as a result of a misrepresentation whether innocent or fraudulent, then he is not bound by the exemption clause.

1. [1940] 1 K.B. 532
2. [1934] 2 K.B. 394

Contract Law

Curtis v Chemical Cleaning Co[3]

X took her wedding dress to be cleaned. She was asked to sign a receipt on which there were conditions by which the cleaners disclaimed liability for damage however it might arise. Before signing X enquired what the effect of the document was and was told that it restricted the cleaner's liability in certain ways and in particular placed on X the risk of damage to beads and sequins on the dress. The dress was badly stained in the course of cleaning. C brought an action for damages. The company raised an exemption clause in their defence.

Held: the cleaners could not rely on their disclaimer since they had misled X as to the effect of the document which she signed.

(d) In case of an ambiguity, the ambiguity is always resolved in favour of the person who is not the maker of the document. This is known as the Contra Proferentum Rule. In particular, if an exemption clause covers negligence, but the terms of the clause are ambiguous and not specific, the Court will construe such a clause against the party relying on it.

Alderslade v Hendon Laundry[4]

The conditions of contracts made by a laundry with its customers excluded liability for loss of or damage to customers clothing in the possession of the laundry. Through its negligence the laundry lost A's handkerchief.

Held: the exclusion clause would have no meaning unless it covered loss due to negligence. Therefore it did cover loss through negligence.

(e) If the contractual document is unsigned the question will be whether reasonable notice of the exemption term has been given. If the notice given is reasonable, the contract is binding.

3. [1951] 1 K.B. 805
4. [1945] K.B. 189

Exemption Clauses

Parker v S E Railway[5]

P deposited a bag in the defendant's cloakroom. He paid 2 pence and was given a ticket on the face of which was printed "See Back". On the back of the ticket was a printed notice saying that the company would not be responsible for any item whose value was more than £10. P's bag, which was worth more than £10, was lost and he brought an action for damages against the company. P had not read the notice on the back of the ticket.

Held: P had notice of the condition on the back of the ticket, the condition was part of a counter-offer by the defendant company which was accepted by P. The printed notice was therefore part of the contract and the company could rely on it in its defence.

(f) An exemption clause will not be binding if it is not brought to the attention of the other party before the contract is made.

Olley v Marlborough Court[6]

H and W arrived at a hotel and paid for a room in advance. On reaching their bedroom they saw a notice on the wall by which the hotel disclaimed liability for loss of valuables unless they are handed to the management for safe-keeping. The wife locked the room and handed the key in at the reception desk. A thief obtained the key and stole the wife's furs from the bedroom.

Held: the hotel could not rely on the notice disclaiming liability since the contract had been made (when the room was booked and paid for) and the disclaimer was too late.

(g) The Court may infer notice of an exemption clause from previous course of dealings between the parties. But it must be a consistent course.

---

5. (1877) 2 C.P.D. 416
6. [1949] 1 K.B. 532

Contract Law

Spurling v Bradshaw[7]
The defendant had dealings for several years with the plaintiff's warehousemen. The defendant delivered to them for storage 8 barrels of orange juice. A few days later the defendant received from them a document acknowledging the receipt of the barrels and referring on its face to clauses printed on the back. One clause exempted the plaintiffs "from any loss or damage due to negligence of themselves or their servants". When the defendant came to collect the barrels, they were found to be empty. The plaintiffs sued the defendant for storage charges but the defendant counter-claimed for negligence and the plaintiffs then pleaded the exemption clause. The defendant argued that, as the document containing exemption clause was sent to him only after the conclusion of the contract, it was too late to affect his rights. But he admitted that in previous dealings he had received a similar document.
Held: defendant was bound by the exemption clause.

(h) If an exemption clause is unusual in a particular type of contract, it must be proved that it has been brought to the notice of the other party.

Thorton v Shoe Lane Parking[8]
P wished to park in the defendants' automatic car park. There was a notice which stated: "All cars parked at owners' risk". As P drove in, a ticket pushed out from the machine. P did not read the ticket. The ticket referred to conditions displayed elsewhere in the car park. P was injured in an accident. On being sued, the defendants claimed that they were protected by the exempting conditions.
Held: the defendants could not rely on the exemption clause because they did not take sufficient steps to draw the attention of the customer to the conditions.
Lord Denning said:
"... the offer was contained in the notice at the entrance giving the charges for garaging and saying

8. [1971] 2 Q.B. 163
7. [1956] 2 All E.R. 121

Exemption Clauses

'at owners risk', that is, at the risk of the owners so far as damage to the car was concerned. The offer was accepted when the plaintiff drove up to the entrance and, by the movement of his car, turned the light from red to green, and the ticket was thrust at him. The contract was then concluded and it could not be altered by any words printed on the ticket itself. In particular, it could not be altered so as to exempt the company from liability for personal injury due to their negligence."

(i) No stranger to a contract can shelter under an exemption clause.

Alder v Dickson[9]

P was a passenger in the P & O Co's vessel. Ticket exempted the company from liability for injuries occasioned by the negligence of the company's servants. P was injured and sued not the company but the master of the ship.
Held: only the company could be protected by the clause and not the third party, i.e, the master of the ship.

2. Statutory Restrictions

There are a number of statutory provisions governing the effectiveness of exemption clauses.

The Unfair Contract Terms Act 1977 (UK) affords a degree of protection to the public in that it makes void any term in a contract seeking to exempt a party from legal liability for any misrepresentation made by him before the contract was signed, unless it is shown that the exemption clause was reasonable.

Section 6(I)(a) of the Unfair Contract Terms Act 1977 (UK) provides that liability for breach of the obligations arising from section 12 of the Sale of Goods Act 1979 (UK) (which deems that the seller has the right to sell the goods) cannot be excluded by reference to any contract term.

In contracts made between businesses and consumers, any term excluding the seller from liability for misdescription of the goods, their merchantable quality and fitness for the purpose s 6 (2) UCTA

9. [1955] 1 Q.B. 158

Contract Law

for which the goods are bought is void under Section 6(i) of the Unfair Contract Terms Act 1977 (UK).

S 6 (3) UCTA

But in non-consumer sales, ie, contracts made between businesses, clauses excluding these terms are valid if shown to be reasonable.

S 2 UCTA

No exclusion clause can restrict or exclude liability for negligence resulting in death or personal injury. But where negligence results in any other type of loss, eg, damage to property, the clause is valid if it is shown to be reasonable.

3. Fundamental Breach and Exemption Clause

Fundamental breach refers to a breach of contract that is so serious that it entitles the other party to put an end to the contract. Fundamental breach is the same as non-performance. The performance of the contract is totally different from that which the parties contemplate.

Suppose X contracts to supply beans but supplies peas instead. There is thus a non-performance of a contract because X has supplied something which is fundamentally different from what he has agreed to deliver.

A breach entitles the innocent party to treat the contract at an end or to affirm the contract.

Doctrine of Fundamental Breach

Where there is a fundamental breach and a party seeks to rely on an exemption clause, it is a matter of construction (legal interpretation) of the contract as to whether such reliance is allowed. This is known as the rule of construction.

For some time,[10] there was a trend towards the view that it was a rule of law that the party in breach could not rely on an exemption clause if there was a fundamental breach. This is the rule of law.

In 1966, in the Suisse Atlantique case,[11] the House of Lords decided *obiter dicta* that the doctrine of fundamental breach is a rule of construction and not a rule of law. The contracting parties are free to agree on the extent of the exemption clauses. Whether these clauses are applicable in a

---

10. Harbutt's Plasticine Ltd v Wayne Tank and Pump Co Ltd [1970] 1 Q.B.447; Wathes Ltd v Austins Ltd [1976] 1 Lloyd's Rep. 14; Karsales (Harrow) Ltd v Wallis [1956] 2 All E.R. 866; Lilley v Doubleday (1881) 7 Q.S.D.510.
11. (1967) 1 A.C. 361

particular situation will depend on their construction. The exemption clauses may be wide enough to cover even a fundamental breach if that is the intention of the parties.

Despite the House of Lord's preference for the rule of construction approach in the Suisse Atlantique case, later Courts, especially the Court of Appeal, showed preference for the rule of law approach.[12]

The law was finally resolved in 1980 in another House of Lords case, Photo Production Ltd v Securicor Transport Ltd.[13] The facts were as follows:

> The plaintiffs contracted with the defendants for the provision of a night patrol service for the plaintiffs' factory. The contract was on the defendants' printed form with standard conditions, including exemption clauses. One of the defendants' employees on patrol lit a fire which burned down the factory. On being sued for damages, the defendants attempted to rely on the exemption clauses which excluded them from responsibility for the employee's act in setting fire to the factory. They contended that the doctrine of fundamental breach did not prevent them from relying on the exemption clauses. The House of Lords took the opportunity to reiterate the principle enunciated in Suisse Atlantique. The conclusion of their Lordships as summarised in the headnotes states:
>
>> "That the question whether and to what extent an exclusion clause was to be applied to any breach of contract was a matter of construction of the contract and normally when the parties were bargaining on equal terms they should be free to apportion the risks as they thought fit, making provision for their respective risks according to the terms they chose to agree."
>
> Their Lordships held that the words of the exemption clause were clear. The construction of the whole contract covered deliberate acts as well as negligence relieving the defendants of responsibility for their breach of the implied duty to operate with due care.

12. Harbutt's Plasticine Ltd Wayne Tank and Pump Co Ltd, supra, and Wathes Ltd v Austins Ltd, supra.
13. (1980) A.C. 827

9 Misrepresentation

In the negotiations leading up to a contract, many statements may be made. Some statements become a term in the main contract and if untrue, there will be a breach of contract. Some statements do not become the terms of any contract and such statements are called "mere representations", and if untrue, do not result in a breach of contract but a misrepresentation. In other words, a non-contractual representation which is untrue is a misrepresentation.

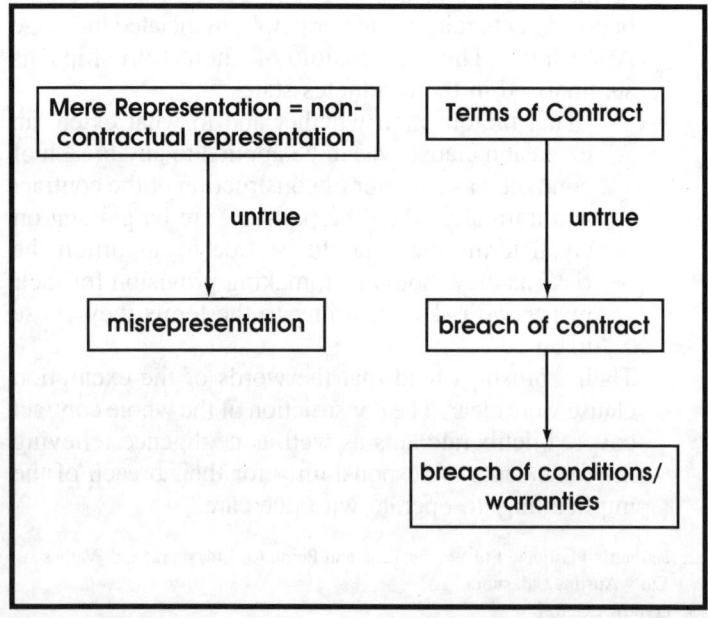

1. What is Misrepresentation?
A misrepresentation is
— a false statement
— of a material fact
— made by one party to another
— which induces the other party to enter into a contract.

A statement of fact which is a representation must be distinguished from a statement of law, from a statement of opinion or intention and from mere vague "sales talk".

Statement of Fact
A misstatement amounts to a misrepresentation only if it is a statement of fact.

A misrepresentation must be on:
Fact, Not Law
If the statement is a statement of law and not of fact it is not a misrepresentation. For example, if a legal principle is wrongly stated there is no misrepresentation.

Fact, Not Opinion
If the statement is a statement of opinion and not of fact, it is not a misrepresentation.

If it is proved that the opinion was not actually held, there is a misrepresentation of fact. But if the opinion was actually held there is no misrepresentation even where the opinion was mistakenly held, as illustrated in the case of Bisset v Wilkinson.[1] The facts were as follows:

> The vendor of a piece of land in New Zealand told a purchaser that, in his opinion, the land would carry 2000 sheep. In fact, the land would not carry that number of sheep.
>
> *Held:* there was no misrepresentation because it was a statement of opinion which was honestly held and was not a statement of fact.

---

1. [1927] A.C. 177

Contract Law

A statement of opinion by someone who should know the facts may amount to a statement of fact because it may be implied that he knows of facts which justify his opinion. This can be seen in the case of Smith v Land & House Property Corporation.[2] The facts were as follows:

> The vendor described his property as being "let to Mr Frederick Fleck — a most desirable tenant". In fact, the tenant was in arrears with his rent.
>
> *Held:* The description of Fleck was not a statement of opinion because the vendor was impliedly stating "that he knows facts which justify his opinion". The statement was an implied assertion that nothing had occured which could make Fleck an undesirable tenant. As a statement of fact this was untrue.

Fact, Not Intention

If the statement is a statement of intention and not of fact it is not a misrepresentation. But a statement of intention may amount to a statement of fact.

Edgington v Fitzmaurice[3]

> The directors of a company iniated a loan from the public and stated that the money would be used to improve the company's building and to expand the business. The real intention of the directors was to use the money to pay off the company's existing debts. Their statement of intention was held to be a statement of fact.

Fact, Not Vague Sales Talk

A statement extolling the virtues of goods which by virtue of its vagueness or extravagance is not a misrepresentation. Thus the statement "very good second-hand reaper" was held to be mere exaggerated sales talk and not a misrepresentation in Chalmers v Harding (1868) 17 L.T. 571.

---

2. (1884) 28 Ch. D. 7
3. (1885) 29 Ch. D. 459

2. Silence as Misrepresentation

The general rule is that mere silence is not misrepresentation. For example, in the case of a contract of sale of goods there is no general duty of disclosure. But in certain cases silence or non-disclosure may amount to misrepresentation. There is a duty to disclose information in the following cases:

(a) Change of Circumstances

Where a statement, true at the time it was made, becomes untrue during the course of negotiations, then there is a duty to disclose.

With v O'Flanagon[4]

>D wanted to sell his medical practice. Negotiations for sale to P began in January when D said that the practice was worth £2,000 a year, which at that time it was. D then fell ill and by May, when the contract of sale was signed, the practice had become worthless.
>
>*Held:* D's silence in the face of this development was a misrepresentation.

(b) The Truth but not the Whole Truth

Where a half-truth amounts to a misrepresentation, then there is a duty to disclose. What is said must be complete to avoid giving a misleading impression.

(c) Contracts of Utmost Good Faith

There is a duty to disclose material facts in contracts of utmost good faith, eg, contracts of insurance. These are contracts in which one party is in a very strong position, having full knowledge of the facts, compared with the other party.

(d) Fiduciary Relationship

Where a fiduciary relationship exists between the contracting parties, then there is a duty of disclosure, eg, contracts between the principal and agent.

---

4. [1936] Ch. 575

Contract Law

3. Inducement

A misstatement is a misrepresentation only if it induces the person to enter into a contract. There is no inducement if one:
- (i) relies on one's own judgment or independent investigations; Attwood v Small[5]

  Vendor offered to sell a mine and made exaggerated statement about its capacity. The buyer appointed expert agents to investigate the mine. The agents reported wrongly that the statements were true. The contract of sale was then completed.

  Held: there was no operative misrepresentation because the buyer had not relied on the vendor's statement, but on his own independent investigations
- (ii) knows of false statement; or
- (iii) never knows of its existence.

A person can sue for misrepresentation if he is given the opportunity to verify the truth but did not do so.

Redgrave v Hurd[6]

A man was induced to buy a solicitor's practice by a misstatement of its value. He was given an opportunity to examine the accounts but did not do so. If he had examined the accounts he would have discovered the truth.

Held: the misstatement was a misrepresentation.

4. Misrepresentation need not be Sole Inducement

If a misstatement is one of the factors that induce a person to enter into a contract, he can claim relief even though there are other inducing factors.

Edgington v Fitzmaurice[7]

P was induced to take debentures in a company, partly by:

---

5. (1838) 6 Cl. & Fin. 232
6. (1881) 20 Ch. D. 1
7. supra.

— a misstatement in the prospectus on how the money was going to be used; and
— his own incorrect belief that the debenture holders would have a charge on the company's property.

Held: the misstatement was an operative misrepresentation.

5. Effect of Misrepresentation
Misrepresentation renders a contract voidable and not void. The contract is valid unless the innocent party, on discovering the misrepresentation, elects to rescind it. The effect of rescission is to nullify the contract *ab initio*, ie, to treat it as if it had never existed.

6. Types of Misrepresentation
There are 3 types of misrepresentation:
    (a) fraudulent misrepresentation;
    (b) negligent misrepresentation; and
    (c) innocent misrepresentation.

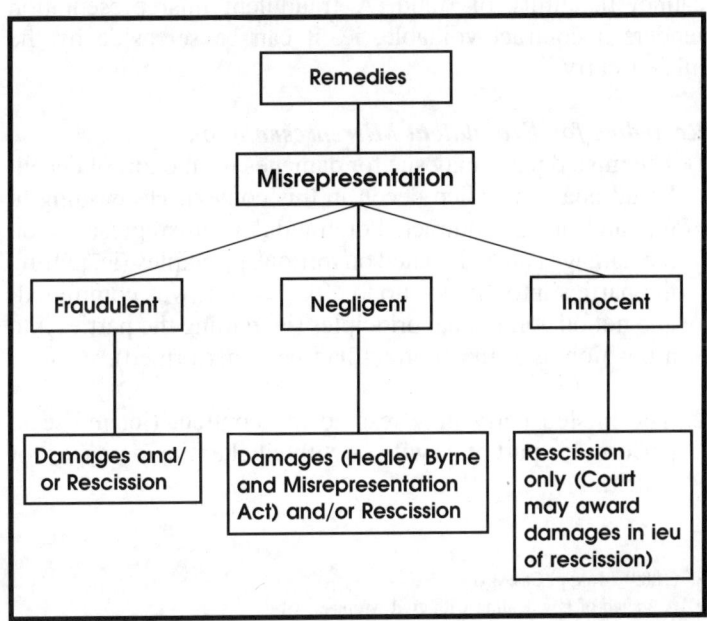

7. Fraudulent Misrepresentation

A false statement is fraudulent if it is made
— knowingly; or
— without belief in its truth; or
— recklessly, careless about whether it be true or false.

Derry v Peek[8]
> D and other directors of a company published a prospectus inviting the public to apply for shares. The prospectus stated that the company had statutory powers to operate trams in Plymouth, drawn by horses or driven by steam power. But the Act required that the company should obtain a licence from the Board of Trade for the operation of steam trams. The directors assumed that the licence would be granted whenever they might apply for it. But it was later refused.
> *Held:* the directors honestly believed that the statement made was true and so this was not a fraudulent misrepresentation.

If the maker believes that his representation is true, he cannot be guilty of fraud. A fraudulent misrepresentation renders a contract voidable, ie, it can be set aside by the misled party.

Remedies for Fraudulent Misrepresentation

1. The misled party may sue for damages for the tort of deceit. Fraud is a tort[9] called deceit in this context. He is suing in tort and not in contract. For fraudulent misrepresentation the damages are calculated on tortious principles (ie, putting the parties into the position before the tort was committed) and not on contractual principles (ie, putting the parties into a position as if the contract had been performed).

2. The misled party may rescind the contract (ie, refuse to perform his part of it) with or without claiming damages for deceit.

---

8. (1889) 14 App. Cas. 337
9. A branch of law dealing with civil wrongs.

3. The misled party may affirm the contract and still claim damages for deceit.

8. Negligent Misrepresentation

Negligent misrepresentation is a statement made in the belief that it is true but without reasonable grounds for that belief.

At one time there was no distinction between negligent misrepresentation and innocent misrepresentation. All non-fraudulent misrepresentations were treated as innocent misrepresentations. And no damages were allowed. The only remedy given was rescission (ie, termination of contract). Two developments altered this position. One was the famous case of Hedley Byrne & Co Ltd v Heller & Partners Ltd[10] and the other was the Misrepresentation Act 1967 (UK). So there is now a distinction between negligent and innocent misrepresentation. There is also a right to damages for negligent misrepresentation.

Negligent Misstatement under Hedley Byrne case

In the leading case of Hedley Byrne v Hellers, the House of Lords held that in some circumstances an action would lie in tort for negligent misstatement. The facts were as follows:

> Hedley Byrne, a firm of advertising agents, wanted to know whether their clients Easipower were creditworthy before Hedley Byrne accepted more advertising orders from them. Hedley Byrne therefore asked their own bank, National Provincial, to make inquiries. National Provincial inquired of Heller & Partners, Easipower's bank, and was told "in confidence and without responsibility on our part" that Easipower were good for I00,000 a year. Relying on that reply, Hedley Byrne placed further orders on behalf of Easipower. Easipower later went into liquidation. Hedley Byrne lost more than I7,000. They sued Heller & Partners for negligence to recover I7,000 as damages.
>
> *Held:* Hedley Byrne's action failed because Heller & Partners' replies were given "without responsibility". But for this disclaimer, an action for negligence would lie.

Where X in the ordinary course of business asks Y for

---

10. [1964] A.C. 465

information, when it is clear that X is relying on Y to exercise a reasonable degree of care in answering and Y knows or ought to have known that X is so relying on him, then Y will be under a duty to take reasonable care. The duty is based on a "special relationship" which must exist between the parties.

Negligent Misrepresentation under Misrepresentation Act 1967 (UK)

<small>S 2(1) MA 1967</small> The Misrepresentation Act 1967 (UK) distinguishes between negligent and innocent misrepresentation and gives a right to damages for negligent misrepresentation.

A person induced to enter into a contract by negligent misrepresentation may sue for damages either under the Hedley Byrne principle or under Section 2(I) of the Misrepr sentation Act 1967 (UK) for any loss.

Hedley Byrne	Misrepresentation Art
– action in tort for negligence – needs "special relationship" – burden of proof on plaintiff to prove negligent misrepresentation	– damages for negligent misrepresentation under Art – no need for "special relationship" – burden of proof on defendant to disprove his negligence

Where the misrepresentor is not a party to the contract, the statutory action under Section 2(1) of the Misrepresentation Act (UK) is not available because Section 2(1) action only applies where a person (ie, misrepresentor) has entered into a contract. Therefore, the misrepresentee can only sue under the principle of Hedley Byrne. Then he must show a "special relationship" between himself and the misrepresentor and he will have to prove negligence.

In addition to, or instead of, suing for damages, the misled party may rescind (ie, terminate) the contract.

Under section 2(2) of the Misrepresentation Act (UK), the Court may award damages instead of rescission.

9. Innocent Misrepresentation
Innocent misrepresentation is a statement made in the belief that it is true and with reasonable grounds for that belief.

The misled party has no right to damages for innocent misrepresentation. (Damages can be demanded only in the case of fraudulent and negligent misrepresentation.) He has the right to rescission only. But the Court has a discretion to award damages instead of rescission.

S 2 (2) MA 1967

10. Rescission
On discovering the misrepresentation, the misled party may elect to affirm or rescind the contract. Rescission is the equitable remedy for all 3 types of misrepresentation.

If the misled party decides to rescind, he must within a reasonable time communicate his decision to the representor that he refuses to be bound by the contract. But if the representor, being a fraud, disappears and it is impossible to find him, the requirement of communication is satisfied if the representee records his intention to rescind by some act that is reasonable in the circumstances.

Car & Universal Finance Co Ltd v Caldwell[11]
> A man was induced by fraud to sell his car to a rogue called Norris. Norris' cheque bounced and Norris disappeared. The owner at once notified the police and the Automobile Association and asked them to find the car. *Held:* by setting the police and the Automobile Association in motion, the owner had sufficiently evinced his intention to rescind the contract. His action successfully avoided the contract.

11. Restitution and Indemnity
Rescission requires *restitutio in integrum*, ie, restoring the parties to their original positions. Thus rescission will involve mutual restitution, ie, "a giving back and taking back on both sides". The principal aim is to put the parties back into their

11. [1961] 1 Q.B. 525

Contract Law

former positions as though the contract had never been made.

A money payment in connection with rescission is called a indemnity to distinguish it from damages. This can be illustrated by the case of Whittington v Seale-Hayne:[12]

> The plaintiffs, poultry breeders, were induced to take a lease of certain premises by the defendant's innocent misrepresentation that the premises were in a sanitary condition. The premises turned out to be very insanitary; the water supply was poisoned. The manager of the poultry farm became ill and most of the poultry died. Moreover, the local council declared the premises unfit for habitation and required the drains to be put in order. In an action for rescission, the plaintiffs claimed for loss of profits, loss of stock, removal expenses and medical expenses.
>
> *Held:* the Court rejected these claims because they were in effect a claim for damages. The plaintiffs' right to an indemnity was limited to rent and rates and costs of repairs ordered by the council.

12. Loss of Right to Rescind

The right to rescind is lost in any of the following circumstances:

(a) Where the contract is affirmed with full knowledge of the facts and of the misrepresentation

Affirmation means intention to proceed with the contract. Lapse of time may be treated as evidence of affirmation.

Leaf International Galleries [13]

> P was induced to buy a picture by an innocent misrepresentation that it was a Constable. Five years later he discovered that it was not by Constable.
>
> *Held:* he lost his right of rescission. He had not affirmed the contract, but his claim was barred by lapse of time.

---

12. (1900) 82 L.T. 49
13. [1950] 2 K.B. 86

(b) Where restitution is impossible
Where the parties cannot be restored to their original positions (ie, pre-contract positions), for example, when the goods sold are consumed or altered by the buyer. But rescission is still available if substantial restoration is possible, even though precise restoration is not. For example, deterioration in the condition of a property is not a bar to rescission. The Court can accompany its order for rescission with financial adjustments between the parties.

c) Where third party's rights are involved
No rescission is possible if a third party acquires right under the contract in good faith and for value.

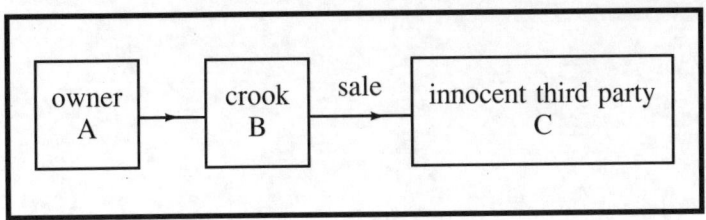

Suppose B obtained goods from A by fraudulent misrepresentation. B sells goods to C who buys in good faith and for value. B never paid A. A seeks to rescind the contract between A and B. A will fail because C obtained property (ie, ownership) under the voidable contract and before that contract is avoided by A, he (ie, C) gets a good title.

13. Misrepresentation and Breach
An untrue statement may start life as a "mere representation" and then later be incorporated into a contract as a "term" of the contract. In such cases, the misled party can still rescind on account of a misrepresentation even though the "misrepresentation" has later become a term of the contract. If it is a term of the contract and proves to be untrue, the misled party may claim damages for breach of contract. If, however, the statement does not become a term of the contract and it is untrue, the misled party may treat it as a misrepresentation and rescind (ie, cancel the contract) and/or recover damages.

S 1 M A 1967

14. Misrepresentation and Exemption Clauses

S 8
UCTA
1977

If a contract contains a term which will exclude or restrict:
    (a) any liability in the case of misrepresentation made by a party before the contract is made; or
    (b) any remedy available to the other party as a result of such misrepresentation,

that term shall have no effect unless it satisfies the test of reasonableness imposed by the Unfair Contract Terms Act 1977 (UK). The requirement of reasonableness applies only to the contract term. The term must be fair and reasonable having regard to the circumstances known to, or in the contemplation of the parties when the contract was made.

10 Duress and Undue Influence

A person who has been induced to enter into a contract by duress or undue influence is entitled to avoid it, ie, the contract is voidable at his option, because he has not given his genuine consent to the contract.

1(A) Duress

Duress is the use or threat of force or of unlawful imprisonment to induce a person to enter into a contract. Duress means actual violence or threats of violence to a person. Persons threatened need not be the contracting party, they may be his wife, parent or child.

Duress is exercised against persons only and not their goods. Threat to the goods of a person is not duress.

Where there is duress, the consent is not freely given and the contract is voidable and may be set aside by the Court.

Cumming v Ince[1]
> An elderly lady was induced to make a settlement of her property in favour of a relative by a threat of unlawful imprisonment in a mental home.
> *Held:* the settlement would be set aside on account of duress.

1(B) Economic Duress

Where a party to a contract is forced by economic pressure to renegotiate the terms of the contract, his apparent consent may be vitiated by duress.

---

1. (1847) 11 Q.B. 112

Atlas Express Ltd v Kafco (Importers and Distributors) Ltd[2]
A, a national road carrier, entered into a contract with K, a small company which imported and distributed basketware to deliver cartons of K's basketware to a national retail chain. A inspected the cartons, which were of different sizes, and agreed at a rate of £1.10 per carton. In fact the first load contained fewer cartons than estimated by A. A then informed K that he would not carry any more cartons unless K agreed to pay a minimum sum per load. K had no choice but to agree to the new terms. A later brought an action to recover the amount owing under the new rate.

Held: A's action amounted to economic duress, and K's apparent consent was vitiated. Claim dismissed.

2. Undue Influence

Undue influence occurs when a person enters into a contract under any kind of influence which prevents him from exercising a free and independent judgment, that is, influencing the mind of the other party so that he cannot arrive at an independent decision. Undue influence renders the contract voidable.

There are 2 classes of undue influence:

(a) No Special Fiduciary Relationship

If there is no special fiduciary relationship between the parties, undue influence must be proved by the victim (ie, the person who was pressed into the contract).

Suppose B (the victim) promises to pay money, B must prove that he was pressed into the promise by a threat that if he did not promise he would be hurt. The burden of proof is on B to show that such an influence existed and was exerted. Equity will not readily presume that there is a fiduciary relationship between parties.

Lai Kwee Lan & Anor v Ng Kew Lan & Anor[3]
The first defendant was a brother of the deceased whose estate was claiming from him return of 50,000 shares in

2. [1989] 1 All E.R. 641
3. [1990] 1 M.L.J. 21

the deceased's company. The first defendant was alleged to have wrongfully acquired the shares from his terminally ill brother who was in hospital. The deceased knew no English and relied on his brother for assistance and interpretation. The first defendant claimed that the shares had been sold to him for $50,000. However the shares were valued at more than that amount and the first defendant was unable to prove that he had paid $50,000 for them.

Held: In the absence of evidence that the first defendant was in a position of active confidence, equity will not presume that a brother in a confidential position and therefore has undue influence over another sibling, not even if it is an elder brother to a younger brother. The plaintiffs were able to prove that there had been no sale as no monies were paid and therefore were able to succeed in their claim.

The court declared that the shares were held by the first defendant for the estate of the deceased by way of resulting or constructive trust.

(b) Special Fiduciary Relationship

When the parties stand in certain relationships the law assumes that one has undue influence over the other. These relationships include the following:

(i) parent and child;
(ii) guardian and ward;
(iii) doctor and patient;
(iv) solicitor and client;
(v) religious adviser and disciple.

These are relationships where one party is the dominant person and it is therefore his duty to prove that there is no undue influence.[4] Examples of undue influence include moral pressure, threats of violence to property and playing on the victims superstitions.

If the dominant party cannot prove the absence of undue influence, the contract will be set aside. To rebut the presumption of undue influence, the dominant party must

---

4. Section 113 of the Evidence Act (Cap 97) 1990 Ed.

show that the victim was not influenced, ie, he exercised his own free will. One way is to show that he had independent advice.

Lloyds Bank v Bundy[5]
A son was in financial difficulty and the bank required additional security for its loan to him. The father gave the bank a charge over his house.
Held: the bank could not itself give independent financial advice to a customer on a matter in which the bank was interested as a creditor. Since the bank had not arranged for the customer to have an independent advice the charge in favour of the bank would be set aside.

3. Right to Relief Lost

A person's right to avoid a contract for undue influence is lost if there is delay in taking action after he has knowledge of his rights.

Allcard v Skinner[6]
Under the influence of a clergyman A entered a Protestant convent and in compliance with a vow of poverty transferred property worth about £7,000 to the order. After 10 years, A left the order and become a Roman Catholic. Six years later she demanded the return of the unexpended balance of her gift.
Held: it was a clear case of undue influence since, among other things, the rules of the order forbade its members to seek advice from any outsider. But A's delay of 6 years (after leaving the order) in making her claim debarred her from setting aside the gift and recovering her property.

5. [1975] Q.B. 326
6. (1887) 36 Ch. D. 145

11 Mistake

The general rule is that a party to a contract is not discharged from his obligations because he is mistaken as to the terms of the contract or the relevant circumstances. Not all mistakes will affect the validity of a contract. Mistakes of the kind that will make a contract void are known as "operative mistakes". An operative mistake is of a serious nature, so serious that it prevents the formation of any contract. There are exceptional and limited categories of "operative mistake" which render the contract void.

Operative mistakes may be common, mutual or unilateral.

1. Common Mistake

Common mistake is where there is complete agreement between the parties but both are equally mistaken as to some fundamental point.

If the parties make a contract relating to a subject-matter which unknown to them both does not exist or which has ceased to exist, there is no contract between them.

Couturier v Hastie[1]
> The contract made in London was for the sale of a cargo of corn shipped from Salonika. Unknown to the parties the cargo had meanwhile been sold by the master of the ship at Tunis since it had begun to rot.
> *Held:* the contract related to a non-existent subject-matter and was void.

---

1. (1856) 5 H.L.C. 673

On similar principles, a policy of life assurance taken out on the life of a person already dead has been held to be void.[2]

Parties may make a common mistake as to the fact or quality of the subject matter which is fundamental to the agreement. This mistaken fact or quality makes the subject matter of the contract essentially different from what they believed it to be. If the mistaken quality is not fundamental, the contract is not void.

The leading modern case in this field is Bell v Lever Bros,[3] the facts of which were as follows:

> L, the controlling shareholder of a Niger company, appointed B to be the managing director of the company for 5 years. Before the 5 years had elapsed B became redundant owing to a merger and L negotiated with B for the cancellation of his service agreement on a payment to B of £30,000. Later L discovered that while serving as managing director B had used inside information to trade in cocoa on his own account. This was serious misconduct for which B might have been summarily dismissed. B was said to have forgotten the significance of his past conduct in negotiating the cancellation of his service agreement, ie, it was treated as a case of common mistake. L's claim to recover £30,000 from B was that there had been a common mistake as to an essential quality of the subject matter, ie, the service agreement for which L had paid £30,000 was in fact valueless to B since he could have been dismissed without compensation.
>
> *Held:* L's claim must fail. It was not a case of non-existent subject matter. If L's claim was correct in its theoretical basis there was not here a sufficiently fundamental mistake as to the "quality" of the subject matter.

Modern opinion is inclined to interpret the decision of Bell v Lever Bros to mean that no mistake as to mere "quality" of the subject matter can ever make the contract void. But equitable relief may sometimes be given.

2. Scott v Coulson [1903] 2 Ch. 249
3. [1932] A.C. 161

Equity intervenes and grants discretionary relief where the mistake is not sufficiently fundamental in the eyes of the Common Law but nevertheless serious. In such cases the contract is voidable but not void (as in cases in which the Common Law doctrine applies).

Solle v Butcher[4]

B granted S the lease of a flat at a yearly rental of £250. Both parties believed erroneously that, as the result of structural alterations, the flat was not subject to rent control. The tenant claimed a declaration that the leasewas under rent control, and the landlord counter-claimed for rescission of the lease on the grounds of a common fundamental mistake.

Held: the lease was subject to rent control. The common mistake of the parties was one of fact and not of law. The lease was therefore voidable at the instance of the landlord.

Grist v Bailey[5]

G bought a house from B for £850. Both parties believed that a tenant who was in occupation of the house was a statutory tenant, whereas he was not protected and could have been compelled to quit on notice. The value of the house, with vacant possession, was £2,250.

Held: the parties were under a common mistake of a fundamental nature. While at common law the contract was not void, equity would grant relief and treat the contract as voidable. The seller was entitled to rescind the contract.

2. Mutual Mistake

Mutual mistake is where the parties are at cross-purposes but each believes that the other agrees with him and does not realise that there is a misunderstanding. The parties are not in agreement because they are not talking about the same thing.

---

4. [1950] 1 K.B. 671
5. [1967] Ch. 532

Such a mistake renders the contract void. The case of Raffles v Wichelhaus[6] illustrates it. The facts were as follows;
> The defendants had agreed to buy cotton due to arrive by the ship *Peerless* from Bombay. Unknown to both parties, there were two ships called *Peerless* sailing from Bombay. The defendants were referring to the one sailing in October and the plaintiffs, the one sailing in December.
> *Held:* the contract was void as the parties were negotiating at cross-purposes.

Scriven Bros v Hindley & Co[7]
> At an auction a buyer bid for 2 lots believing both to be hemp. In fact one lot was a mixed batch of hemp and tow. It was not normal practice to sell hemp and tow together and the sale particulars were confusing. The auctioneer was unaware of the buyer's mistake and had not said anything which induced it.
> *Held:* in the circumstances there was no agreement by which the buyer was bound to accept the mixed hemp and tow.

3. Unilateral Mistake

Unilateral mistake is where one party is mistaken and the other who may have induced the mistake is aware of it. Most of the case-law on unilateral mistake is concerned with mistake of identity.

Thus a contract is void for mistake by the seller about the buyer's identity if the seller intends to sell to someone different from the actual buyer. If that is the position, the seller never intends to sell to the actual buyer and the contract with him is void.

The parties may negotiate the contract by correspondence without meeting face to face. If the buyer assumes the identity of another person known to the seller, with whom the seller intends to make the contract, the sale to the actual buyer is void.

6. (1864) 2 H. & C. 906
7. [1913] 3 K.B. 56

Cundy v Lindsay[8]
Blenkarn, a dishonest person, wrote to C from "37 Wood St, Cheapside" to order goods and signed the letter so that his name appeared to be "Blenkiron & Co", a respectable firm, known to C, with their offices at 123 Wood St. The goods were consigned to Blenkiron & Co at 37 Wood St. Blenkarn re-sold the goods to L. C sued L for conversion to recover the value of the goods (for which L had already paid Blenkarn in good faith).
Held: C intended to sell only to B & Co and no title passed to Blenkarn. The mistake over the Wood St address was reasonable. The contract between C and Blenkarn was void. L was liable to C for the value of the goods.

In a situation like the above, the innocent third party suffers. To mitigate the harshness the Court has made a distinction between:
— mistake as to identity (void);
— mistake as to attributes (voidable).

The former results in a void contract while the latter, a voidable contract. It is difficult to differentiate between identity and attributes.

King's Norton Metal Co Ltd v Edridge, Merrett & Co Ltd[9]
Wallis, by using the name of "Hallam & Co", obtained goods on credit. There was no such firm. Wallies sold the goods to the defendants. The plaintiffs sued the defendants to recover damages. The Court held that the plaintiffs had not made a mistake as to the identity of the rogue. They had intended to contract with the writer of the letter and the mistake is on creditworthiness which is an attribute. The contract was voidable for fraud but since it had not been avoided at the time the goods were sold to the defendants by Wallis, the defendants had a good title.

8. (1878) 3 App. Cas. 459
9. (1897) 14 T.L.R. 98

When the parties meet face to face it is generally inferred that the seller intends to sell to the person whom he meets. The latter may mislead the seller as to the buyer's creditworthiness by assuming a false identity.

Phillips v Brooks[10]

A rogue entered a jeweller's shop, selected various items which he wished to buy and proposed to pay by cheque. The jeweller replied that delivery must be delayed until the cheque had been cleared. The rogue then said that he was Sir George Bullough, a well-known person, and the jeweller checked that the real Sir G.B. lived at the address given by the rogue. The rogue then asked to take a ring away with him and the jeweller accepted his cheque and allowed him to have it. The rogue pledged the ring to the defendant, a pawnbroker, who was sued by the jeweller to recover the ring.
Held: the action must fail. There was no mistake of identity which made the contract void but only a mistake as to the creditworthiness of the buyer.

Lewis v Avery[11]

The plaintiff advertised his car for sale and a rogue calling himself Richard Green, a famous actor, responded. He paid by cheque and took the car. Later, he sold the car to the defendant. The cheque was worthless and the rogue was not Richard Green. The rogue disappeared with the money and could not be traced. The plaintiff sued, claiming that the car was still his. Lord Denning M.R. said:

"When a deal is made between a seller like Mr Lewis and a person who is actually there present before him, then the presumption in law is that there is a contract even though there is a fraudulent impersonation by the buyer representing himself as a different man than he is. There is a contract made with the very person there, who is present in person.

---

10. [1919] 2 K.B. 243
11. [1972] 1 Q.B. 198

It is liable no doubt to be avoided for fraud but it is still a good contract under which title will pass unless and until it is avoided."

Thus the contract was made with the rogue who was physically present before the seller and not with Richard Green. Since the rogue obtained a voidable title to the car and it was sold to the defendant before the contract between the plaintiff and the rogue had been avoided, the defendant obtained a good title.

If a person is deceived by another actually present before him, the contract is normally only voidable, as in Lewis v Avery. But exceptionally, the contract may be void for mistake in similar circumstances, as in the case of Ingram v Little.[12] Ingram's case is inconsistent with the others and it is unlikely to be followed now. The facts of the case were as follows:

Ingram v Little
> I and her two sisters were joint owners of a car which they advertised for sale. X bought it and began to write out a cheque for the price. I told X that the sale was for cash, that the owners were not prepared to accept a cheque and that the sale was cancelled. X replied that he was H, a reputable businessman, giving an address which was checked by one of I's sisters. I believed X to be H and let him have the car in exchange for his cheque. X had nothing to do with H and the cheque was dishonoured. The car was acquired by L in good faith and for value.
> *Held:* the owners intended to sell their car only to H and their offer was only addressed to him; X was incapable of accepting the offer and the owners could recover the car from L.

4. Mistake over Documents

The general rule is that a person is bound by a document that he signs even though he does not read it or does not understand its contents. But there is an exception to this rule—a plea of

---

12. [1961] 1 Q.B.. 31

Contract Law

non est factum, ie, "it is not his deed". If a person signs a contract in the mistaken belief that he is signing a document of a fundamentally different character, there will be mistake which renders the contract void. The mistaken party can successfully plead non est factum. This plea is available in 2 circumstances:
— when the person signing is blind or illiterate;
— when the person is induced to sign the document through fraud.

The party pleading the defence of *non est factum* must also establish that:
— the document signed is fundamentally or essentially different in substance or in kind from what the signer believes it to be; and
— the mistake must have been made without carelessness on the part of the person who signs.

Saunders v Anglia Building Society[13]

Mrs Gallie, a widow of 78, agreed to help her nephew, Parkin, to raise money on the security of her house provided that she continued to live in it until her death. Parkin did not wish to appear in the transaction himself since he feared that his wife, from whom he was separated, would then enforce against him her claim for maintenance. Parkin therefore arranged that Lee, a solicitor's clerk, should prepare the mortgage. As a first step Lee produced a document which was in fact a transfer of the house on sale to Lee. However, Lee told Mrs Gallie that the document was a deed of gift to Parkin and she signed it at a time when her spectacles were broken and she could not read. Lee then mortgaged the house and his property to a building society. Lee paid nothing to Mrs Gallie or to Parkin. Mrs Gallie sought to repudiate the document as *non est factum*. During the progress of the case to the House of Lords the original title (Gallie v Lee) of the case was changed partly because of the death of Mrs Gallie, and Saunders became her executor.

---

13. [1971] A.C. 1004

Held: Mrs Gallie knew that she was transferring her house and her act in signing the document during a temporary inability to read amounted to carelessness. The claim to repudiate the transfer failed. Mrs Gallie could not plead *non est factum*.

Foster v Mackinnon[14]

M, an elderly man of feeble sight was asked to sign aguarantee. He had done so before. The document put before him to sign was actually a bill of exchange which he signed as acceptor. The bill was later negotiated to the plaintiff. M, when sued, repudiated it as *non est factum*.

Held: the document signed was so different from what it was believed to be that a defence of *non est factum* could be available.

5. Rectification of Written Agreements

A type of relief called rectification may be claimed when the document does not correctly record the common intention of the parties. The purpose of rectification is to bring the written contract into conformity with the actual agreement reached.

The party seeking rectification as relief must show that:
— the parties have reached complete agreement;
— the written document did not correspond with the agreement reached.

Joscelyne v Nissen[15]

The plaintiff and the defendant agreed orally that the latter would take over his car-hire business on the understanding that the defendant would pay all the household expenses. In the written agreement, there was no record that the defendant was liable to pay the household expenses. When she ultimately refused to pay electricity, gas and coal bills, the plaintiff brought an action for the document to be rectified to include the defendant's liability for these bills. Rectification was ordered by the Court.

14. (1869) L.R.4 C.P. 704
15. [1970] 2 Q.B. 86

12 Illegal Contracts

Contracts are illegal if they are forbidden by law. Contracts may be unlawful according to Common Law or by statute.

1. Contracts Prohibited by Statute

An Act of Parliament may prohibit a particular type of contract. Such contracts would be illegal and void. An example of a contract forbidden by statute is a gaming or wagering contract (ie, a gambling contract). Gaming refers to a contract involving a game such as a horse-race. Wagering refers to a bet on anything other than a game. A wagering contract is an agreement between 2 parties that upon the happening of some uncertain future event, one party shall pay money to the other depending on the issue of the event. There is no other interest in the contract than winning or losing.

2. Contracts Illegal at Common Law

Certain contracts are illegal because they offend public policy (ie, injurious to society). The following contracts are considered illegal at Common Law on grounds of public policy:

(a) *A Contract to Commit a Crime or Tort*

A contract whose object is the commission of a crime or tort is illegal and void. For example, it is illegal for 2 highwaymen to agree to share the proceeds to be obtained by robbing a coach. Such a contract is illegal so that one highwayman cannot sue the other for his share.[1]

---

1. Everet v Williams (1725) 9 L.Q.R. 197

(b) A Contract Tending to Promote Sexual Immorality

If the common purpose of the contract is to promote sexual immorality, the contract is illegal and void. Thus in the leading case of Pearce v Brooks,[2] a firm of coach builders knowingly hired out a carriage to a prostitute to further her trade. When the prostitute fell into arrears, they sued to recover the debt. The Court rejected the claim because it was a contract to further an immoral trade.

In another case of Upfill v Wright,[3] the landlord let a flat to a woman, a mistress of a certain man. The landlord knew that the man gave money to the mistress for the rent "as the price of her immorality". The landlord sue for the rent and failed because the flat was let for an immoral purpose. The contract was held by the Court to be illegal.

(c) A Contract Prejudicial to Public Security

Such a contract would be, for example, a trading contract made in times of war with an enemy and is illegal.

(d) A Contract Prejudicial to the Administration of Justice

Contracts interfering with the course of justice are illegal. For example, a contract to stifle a criminal prosecution, ie, a contract not to prosecute but to compromise a prosecution.

The enforcement of criminal law is a matter of public interest. Thus it is unlawful for A to agree not to prosecute B if B will return the money that he has robbed A of.

(e) A Contract Tending to Promote Corruption in Public Life

Public life refers to the affairs of the country. Any contract that leads to corruption in the administration of the affairs of the country is illegal and void. Thus an agreement amounting to bribery is illegal.

Parkinson v College of Ambulance Ltd[4]

The plaintiff gave the charitable organisation a sum of

---

2. (1866) L.R. 1 Ex 213
3. [1911] 1 K.B. 506
4. [1925] 2 K.B. 1

money as donation because the secretary of the organisation had intimated to him that he could use his influence to secure a knighthood for him. When no title was forthcoming, the plaintiff wanted his money back. *Held:* the plaintiff could not recover. Lush J ruled:
> "the contract, in my opinion, is one that could not be sanctioned or recognized in a court of justice a contract for the purchase of a title, however the money is to be expended, is itself an improper contract."

(f) A Contract to Defraud the Revenue
If the intention of the contracting parties is to defraud the revenue, the contract is unlawful. For example, defrauding the tax authorities or evading the provisions of any tax statutes.

3. Consequences of Illegal Contracts

It is a general rule that no party may claim on an illegal contract. This is expressed in the Latin maxim *"ex turpi causa non oritur actio"* (No action can be brought by a party to an illegal contract). The Court will not assist a party to recover where the cause of action is founded upon an illegal act. Thus, no action can lie for the breach of an illegal contract or for the recovery of property transferred or money paid under an illegal contract.

There are several exceptions to the general rule that the Court will not help in an illegal contract. A party to an illegal contract may recover money paid or property transferred in the following cases:

(a) Where the plaintiff can establish his case without relying on the illegal contract, ie, where he can establish an independent cause of action

For example, in a lease for 5 years, the property being used for immoral purposes with the knowledge of the landlord, the landlord cannot claim possession. After the expiry of the lease period, the landlord can claim possession by virtue of his ownership.

Illegal Contracts

(b) Where the parties are not equally at fault, ie, not in pari delicto

For example, where one of the parties is induced to enter into the illegal contract by the fraudulent conduct of the other.

Hughes v Liverpool Victoria Legal Friendly Society[5]

A grocer insured the lives of customers who owed him money. This was legal since he had an insurable interest. The policies lapsed and an insurance agent persuaded the grocer's wife to take them up, assuring her that this was lawful. It was illegal since she was not their creditor and had no insurable interest. On discovering that the policies were void she sued to recover the premiums paid.

Held: she might recover her money since she had been persuaded by fraud to enter into an illegal contract.

(c) Where a plaintiff repents before the contract has been substanially performed

An example of this is where money is deposited with a stakeholder under an illegal contract. Thus entrance fees paid to the organisers of a missing-word competition is recoverable so long as the money has not been paid out to the winner. In such a case the contract is held not to be substantially performed until the money has been paid over to the winner, and therefore the party may retract at any time before that has been done (Hastelow v Jackson (1828) 8 B & C 221 at 226-227).

4. Void Contracts

Void contracts do not give rise to rights and obligations and the full consequences of illegality are not present. Different writers classify illegal contracts differently. Illegal contracts are the more serious examples of "illegality", ie, patently reprehensible and so obviously contrary to public policy. Void contracts are the less serious examples of "illegality", for example, contracts in restraint of trade, contracts to oust the Court's jurisdiction and contracts that tend to prejudice the status of marriage.

---

5. [1916] 2 K.B. 482

Contracts may be void by statute or at Common Law on the grounds of public policy.

(a) Contracts Rendered Void by Statute
All gaming and wagering contracts are null and void. No action can be brought in any court for recovering any money alleged to have been won on any wager. Any money paid under gaming or wagering contracts are also not recoverable.

(b) Contracts Void on the Grounds of Public Policy
There are 3 types of contract that offend public policy which the Court treats as void and not as illegal. These are:
    (i) Contracts to oust the jurisdiction of courts;
    (ii) Contracts prejudicial to the status of marriage; and
    (iii) Contracts in restraint of trade

(i) Contracts to Oust the Court's Jurisdiction
The Court is the final arbiter on questions of law. This jurisdiction cannot be ousted by any agreement between the parties. That is, you cannot bind yourself to refrain from submitting questions of law to the Court.

An arbitration clause by itself does not at common law oust the jurisdiction of the Court. But if the parties seek by an arbitration agreement to take the law out of the hands of the courts and into the hands of an arbitrator, then the agreement, to the extent that it deprives recourse to the courts in case of errors of law, is contrary to public policy.

(ii) Contracts Prejudicial to the Status of Marriage
Contracts in restraint of marriage are void. For example, a contract by a party undertaking not to marry at all is void.

(iii) Contracts in Restraint of Trade
Contracts in restraint of trade are contracts restricting the liberty of a man to carry on his trade, business or profession in any manner he chooses. Contracts in restraint of trade are not illegal but prima facie (on the face of it) void as being against public policy. They will be valid if they are shown to be:
    — reasonable as between both parties; and
    — reasonable as regards the interest of the public.

Illegal Contracts

Test of Valid Restraint
In considering what is reasonable, the Court will take into consideration the circumstances of each case, for example, the length of time of the restraint and the physical area of restraint.

To be reasonable, the restraint must protect and protect only some proprietary or other legitimate interest of the promisee. That is, the restraint must be no wider than is necessary to protect the proper interest of the promisee. Consequently, the restraint must not be excessive as regards its area, time of operation or the trades which it forbids.

If a restraint is void the remainder of the contract by which the restraint is imposed is usually valid and binding, ie, it is merely the restraint which is struck out as invalid.

The doctrine of restraint of trade does not apply to every contract restricting a man's liberty to trade. Certain restrictions are accepted as part of our modern pattern of trade and the Court will usually not nullify them. Therefore, it does not apply to restrictions which are part of the "accepted and normal currency of commercial or contractual relations".

Examples of contracts in restraint of trade are:
— contract of employment;
— sale of goodwill of business;
— solus trading agreements.

5. Restraint in a Contract of Employment
In a contract of employment, an employee may undertake to refrain from carrying on a trade or profession for a certain period or a specified area on leaving his employment. Such a contract is prima facie void unless it can be shown that the restraint is reasonable as between the parties and in the public interest. The restraint is never reasonable unless there is some proprietary interest of the employer which requires protection, eg, trade secrets and business connection. The restraint will be invalid if it gives more protection than necessary. Thus an employee who has access to trade secrets such as manufacturing processes or even financial and commercial information which is confidential may be restrained to prevent him from using them after leaving his present job.

Foster v Suggett[6]
    As works manager S had access to the technical "know-how" of his employer's business of making glass bottles. His contract of employment provided that for 5 years after leaving his employer's service he would not carry on or be interested in the manufacture of glass bottles in the UK or other glass making similar to that of his employer's business.
    Held: it must be shown (and in this case it had been) that the employee had access to secret manufacturing process. The restraint was reasonable and valid.

The restraint is only valid if the nature of the employee's duties gives him knowledge of the affairs or requirements of customers such that if he leaves to take up other work they might follow him because of his knowledge as distinct from his personal skill.

Fitch v Dewes[7]
    A solicitor's clerk at Tamworth agreed that after leaving his employer, he would not for the rest of his life practise as a solicitor within 7 miles of Tamworth Town Hall.
    Held: the restraint was valid since the clerk's knowledge of the affairs of his employer's clients should not be used to the detriment of the employer.

Whether restraint is reasonable or not will depends on the:
    — nature and extent of trade;
    — area covered by the restraint;
    — time period of the restraint.

Area must not be Excessive
The physical area covered by the restraint clause must not be excessive. Whether it is excessive or not depends on the circumstances of each case.

---

6. (1918) 35 T.L.R. 87
7. [1921] 2 A.C. 158

Illegal Contracts

Duration must not be Excessive
The restraint will be void if it is too long in duration. In Fitch v Dewes, the restraint for life was held valid. But in modern times a restriction unlimited in time might well be treated as excessive.

6. Restraint in a Contract of Sale of Business
Unlike contracts in restraint of employment, the Court is more likely to uphold this type of restraint. Buyers of business would not be forthcoming if they (buyers) could not get protection against competition by the vendor. Who would buy a grocer's shop if the vendor was free to set up a new grocer's shop next door? Such restraint is valid only if it is connected with the proprietary interest which has been bought. In other words, the party seeking to enforce the restraint must be able to show that there is some proprietary interest to be protected and it is no wider than is necessary. The Court will take into consideration the question of time and area, ie, whether the time and area are reasonable.

British Concrete Co v Schelff[8]

> S carried on a small local business of making one type of road reinforcement. He sold his business to BC which carried on business throughout the UK in making a range of road reinforcements. S undertook not to compete with BC in the sale or manufacture of road reinforcements.
>
> *Held:* the restraint was void since it was widely drawn to protect BC from any competition by S. In buying the business of S, BC was only entitled to protect what they bought, ie, a local business making one type of product and not the entire range produced by BC in the UK.

7. Solus Trading Agreements
Distributor or supplier agreements are valid since the supplier and distributor bargain in a position of equal strength. In the petrol trade the major suppliers are very large international oil

---

8. [1921] 2 Ch. 563

companies and the distributors are small-scale petrol filling stations. The distributor accepts restrictive conditions. Agreements by which the proprietors of petrol filling stations agree (in consideration of a lump sum payment or other commercial advantages) to purchase all their petrol, etc, requirements from one supplier are valid only if the duration of the agreements is not excessive. It is accepted that the supplier is entitled to acquire and enforce monopoly rights of supply.

It is common for oil companies to enter into "solus" agreements with garage owners. Such arrangements are reasonable between the parties.

Esso Petroleum Co v Harper's Garage[9]

H had 2 petrol filling stations and had agreed to purchase all its petrol supplies for both stations from E. In consideration of this undertaking E agreed to grant a rebate of 1d per gallon on the normal price and to make a loan of £7,000 to H, secured by a mortgage over one of the filling stations. For one filling station the monopoly rights of E were to last for $4^1/_2$ years and for the other (by the terms of the mortgage) for 21 years. The mortgage could not be paid off in less than 21 years. H broke its undertaking and E sued to enforce it.
Held: in both cases a personal restraint of trade had been imposed on H. It was not merely a restriction on the use of land (even though the longer restriction was imposed by a mortgage). Both must be examined under the principles of restraint of trade since arrangements of this kind (unlike some exclusive distributor agreements) were not to be regarded as reasonable by their nature alone. Solus agreements of this type were, however, reasonable if limited to a short period of years. The $4^1/_2$ year restriction was valid but the 21-year restriction on the second filling station was void.

---

9. [1968] A.C. 269

13 Discharge of Contracts

A party may be discharged from his contractual obligations in any of the following ways:
— performance
— agreement
— frustration
— breach

Discharge means the parties are freed from their contractual obligations.

1. Discharge by Performance

This is the normal method of discharge. As a general rule, contractual obligations are discharged only by complete and exact performance. When both parties have performed their obligations, the contract is discharged, ie, the contract is at an end. Thus, in a contract to deliver 100 tons of rubber, this precise amount must be delivered for the contract to be discharged by performance.

This rule requiring complete performance sometimes leads to unjust results. One result of this strict rule is that a party who has only partially performed his obligations cannot recover anything for the work he has done. In other words, partial performance does not suffice nor does incorrect performance.

The case of Cutter v Powell[1] illustrates the unhappy result of this strict general rule. The facts were as follows:

> P employed C as second mate of a ship sailing from Jamaica to Liverpool at a wage of 30 guineas for the

---

1. (1795) 6 Term. Rep. 320

complete voyage. C died at sea when he had completed about three-quarters of the voyage. C's widow sued for aproportionate part of the agreed sum.
Held: C was entitled to nothing unless he completed the voyage.

The Exceptions
This general rule that "performance to be effective must be complete performance" is subject to 4 exceptions.

(a) Divisible Contracts
The rule that the "party who has not completely fulfilled his obligations cannot recover anything for work done" applies when the contract is entire, not when it is divisible.

Cutter v Powell is an example of an entire contract. Thus nothing was to be paid unless P had performed his entire duty under the contract.

A contract may provide for performance by instalments with separate payment for each of them. This is known as a "divisible contract". Where a contract is divisible, payment for parts which have been completed can be claimed.

In the case of Roberts v Havelock[2] there was a divisible contract "to put the ship into thorough repair" and the shipwright was allowed to recover part payment before he completed the work.

(b) Prevention of Performances
If a party to a contract is prevented by the fault of the other party from completing the work, then he can

— sue on a *quantum meruit* (as much as he has deserved) for work done and so be paid a reasonable remuneration for work done;
— sue for damages for breach of contract.

The distinction between a *quantum meruit* claim and a claim for damages is that the former is a claim for reasonable remuneration while the latter is a claim for compensation for a loss.

2. (1832)

Discharge of Contracts

The leading authority is the case of Planche v Colburn,[3] the facts of which were as follows:

> P agreed to write a book to be published by D in a series. P was to be paid £100 on completion of the book. He collected material and wrote part of the book. D then abandoned the series.
> *Held:* P was awarded £50 on a *quantum meruit* claim (as much as he had earned).

(c) Acceptance of Partial Performance

If one party partially performs his obligations and the other party accepts the work, then it is possible to infer a fresh agreement by the parties that payment be made for work already done. In other words, where partial performance is accepted, so that promise to pay is inferred, a claim can be made on a *quantum meruit* to recover remuneration for work done. For example, A orders a dozen bottles of beer from B. B delivers 9 which is all he has in stock. A may reject the 9 bottles but if he accepts them he must pay for 9 bottles at the contract rate.

Such a new promise to pay for partial performance will be inferred only where the beneficiary has a genuine choice whether to accept or reject the benefit of work done. The position where there is no option or genuine choice to reject or accept and therefore no right to sue on a *quantum meruit* is well illustrated by Sumpter v Hedges[4] the facts of which were as follows:

> S undertook to erect buildings on the land of H for a price of £565. S abandoned the work when it was only 60 per cent completed. H completed the work using materials left on his land by S.
>
> S sued for (i) the value of his materials and (ii) the value of his work in so far as it had not already been paid for.
> *Held:* H must pay for the materials since he had elected to use them. But H had no obligation to pay the unpaid balance of the charges for work done by S before abandoning it. H had no choice between accepting or

3. (1831) 8 Bing. 14
4. [1898] 1 Q.B. 673

rejecting the white elephant. No new implied promise to pay could arise from the mere fact that H had reoccupied his own land and gone on with the building.

(d) Substantial Performance

A party who performs his obligations defectively, but substantially, can enforce the contract. In other words, where a contract is substantially performed, the party can sue for the contract price less an abatement for deficiencies.

Hoenig v Issacs[5]

I employed H to decorate I's flat at a total price of £750, to be paid as the work progressed. After paying £400 I objected to the quality of the work and refused to pay the balance for the completed work. The cost of putting right incomplete or defective work was assessed at the trial at £56.

Held: H had made substantial performance. I must pay the balance owing of the total price of £750 less an allowance of £56.

2. Discharge by Agreement

A contractual obligation may be discharged by agreement. Such an agreement must be under seal or supported by consideration.

If the parties enter into a new contract to replace the unperformed contract, the new contract provides any necessary consideration. This is called "novation" of the old contract, ie, its replacement by a new one.

Suppose X agrees to sell a car to Y. Subsequently, both parties decide to call off the deal. Here the contract is discharged by mutual waiver. The parties may also decide to extinguish the original contract and substitute for it a new agreement. This is called novation.

---

5. [1952] 2 All E.R. 176

An example of novation is the case of

Panachand & Co. (Pte) Ltd v Riko International Pte Ltd [6]
R sold to P 543 bags of Cummin seeds for a sum of $75,051.60 on January 13 1981. P paid R a sum of $67,545.90, claiming $7,505.70 as a discount.

In January 20 1982 an associate company of P sold 188 bags of turkish Gallnuts to R for a sum of $53,942.40 The invoice was by mistake made out in the name of P. However this mistake was accepted by R who duly paid out to P a sum of $46,438.70 contending that they were entitled to a set-off for $7,505.70.
Held: When R paid to P the sum of $46,438.70 both parties must have taken to have agreed that the contract was now made between P and R. It was therefore a novation of the contract. Hence P was able to claim for the sum of $7,505.70 as R had failed to make out its defence of a set-off.

3. Discharge by Frustration

The general rule is that a contractual obligation is absolute. The severity of this rule is mitigated by the doctrine of frustration.

Under the doctrine of frustration, the parties are excused further performance of their obligations if some event occurs during the currency of the contract, without the fault of either party,
— which makes further performance impossible or illegal; or
— which makes it something radically different from what was originally undertaken.

When Frustration Occurs
There is frustration when:
(i) the whole basis of the contract is the continued existence of a specific thing which is destroyed.

---

6. [1986] 1 M.L.J. 294

Taylor v Caldwell [7]
>A hall was let for a series of concerts on specified dates. Before the date of the first concert the hall was destroyed by fire. The concert organiser sued the owner of the hall for damages for failure to let him have the use of the hall as agreed.
>*Held:* the destruction of the subject matter (the hall) rendered the contract as impossible to perform and discharged the contract.

(ii) there is personal incapacity (eg, one party dies or becomes ill) to perform a contract of personal service.

Condor v Barron Knights [8]
>C, aged 16, contracted to perform as drummer in a pop group. His duties, when the group had work, were to play on every night of the week. He fell ill and his doctor advised him to restrict his performance to 4 nights per week. The group terminated his contract.
>*Held:* a contract of personal service is based on the assumption that the employee's health will permit him to perform his duties. If that is not so the contract is discharged by frustration. But not every illness discharges a contract of personal service and permanent incapacity must be established.

(iii) the whole basis of the contract is an event which does not occur.

Krell v Henry [9]
>A room overlooking the route of the coronation procession of Edward VII was let for the day of the coronation for the purpose of viewing the procession. The coronation was postponed owing to the illness of the King. The owner of the rooms sued for the agreed fee.
>*Held:* the contract was made for the sole purpose of viewing the procession. As that event did not occur the contract was frustrated.

7. (1836) 3 B. & 5. 826
8. [1966] 1 W.L.R. 87
9. [1903]2 K.B. 740

(iv) there is government intervention or supervening illegality.

Re Shipton[10]
> The contract was for the sale of wheat stored in a Liverpool warehouse. It was requisitioned by the government under emergency wartime legal powers.
> *Held:* it was no longer lawful for the seller to deliver the wheat. The contract had been discharged.
> Supervening illegality, eg, due to outbreak of war or government intervention to restrain or suspend performance of the contract, is a common course of frustration.

4. Limits to Doctrine of Frustration
A contract is not discharged by frustration in the following circumstances:

(a) if one party has induced frustration by his own choice between alternatives
The parties cannot rely on self-induced frustration. In other words, the doctrine of frustration will not apply where the event was induced by one of the parties.

Maritime National Fish v Ocean Trawlers[11]
> Contract for the hire of a trawler for use in otter trawling. The hirers had 4 other trawlers of their own. They applied to the Canadian government for the necessary licences for 5 trawlers but were granted only 3 licences. They nominated 3 of their own trawlers for the licences and argued that the contract for hire of a fifth trawler had been frustrated since it could not be lawfully used.
> *Held:* the impossibility of performing the hire contract was the result of a choice made by the hirers, ie, the trawler on hire could have been nominated for one of the three licences. This was not a case for discharge by frustration.

---
10. [1915] 3 K.B 676
11. [1935] A.C. 524

(b) if an alternative mode of performance is still possible

Tsakiroglou & Co v Noblee and Thor G.m.b.H.[12]
Contract for sale of 300 tons of Sudan groundnuts c.i.f. Hamburg. The normal and intended method of shipment from Port Sudan was by a ship routed through the Suez Canal to Hamburg. Before shipment the Suez Canal was closed; the sellers refused to ship the cargo, arguing that it was an implied term that shipment should be via Suez or, alternatively, that shipment via the Cape of Good Hope would make the contract "commercially and fundamentally" different so that it was discharged by frustration.
Held: both arguments failed. There was no evidence to support the implied term argument nor was the use of a different (and more expensive) route an alteration of the fundamental nature of the contract sufficient to discharge it by frustration.

(c) if performance became unexpectedly more expensive

Davis Contractors v Fareham UDC[13]
DC agreed to build 78 houses at a price of £94,000 in 8 months. Labour shortages caused the work to take 22 months and cost £115,000. DC wished to claim frustration so that they could then claim for their work on a quantum meruit basis.
Held: hardship, material loss or inconvenience did not amount to frustration; the obligation must change such that the thing undertaken would, if performed, be a different thing from that contracted for.

5. Effect of Frustration

When a contract is frustrated it comes to an end. The contract is automatically terminated as to the future. The contract is not void *ab initio*, ie, not void from the beginning. It starts life as a valid contract but automatically comes to an end when the common adventure is frustrated.

12. [1962] A.C. 93
13. [1956] A.C. 696

Discharge of Contracts

The effect of this is that any obligation already due before the frustration must be performed. The parties are excused from performing those obligations which arise subsequent to the frustration. S 3(5) FCA

Suppose Tang has spent a large sum of money building a house for Tay. The house is destroyed by a fire. Tang will have to bear the loss.

This principle causes hardship to Tang. The harshness of the rule is now mitigated by the Law Reform (Frustrated Contracts) Act (Cap. 33). The effects of frustration are now governed by the Law Reform (Frustrated Contracts) Act which changed the Common Law position of the loss lying where it fell:

(a) the contract is discharged as to the future;
(b) money paid in pursuance of the contract before it is frustrated may be recovered;
(c) any sum payable at the time of frustration ceases to be payable; S 2(2) FCA

However, if the party to whom the money is paid has incurred expenses before the frustration for the purpose of performing the contract, the Court may allow him to retain or recover an amount not exceeding the expenses incurred "if it considers it just to do so having regard to all the circumstances".

(d) if one party has enjoyed a valuable benefit before the discharge, the Court may order him to pay to the other party an appropriate sum not exceeding the value of the benefit. S 2(3) FCA

If, for example, one party has delivered to the other some of the goods to be supplied under the contract, the latter may be ordered to pay the amount of their value to him.

However, the Law Reform (Frustrated Contracts) Act does not apply to various special types of contract such as contract for the carriage of goods by sea, contracts of insurance and contracts for the supply of specific goods if frustrated by the perishing of the goods.

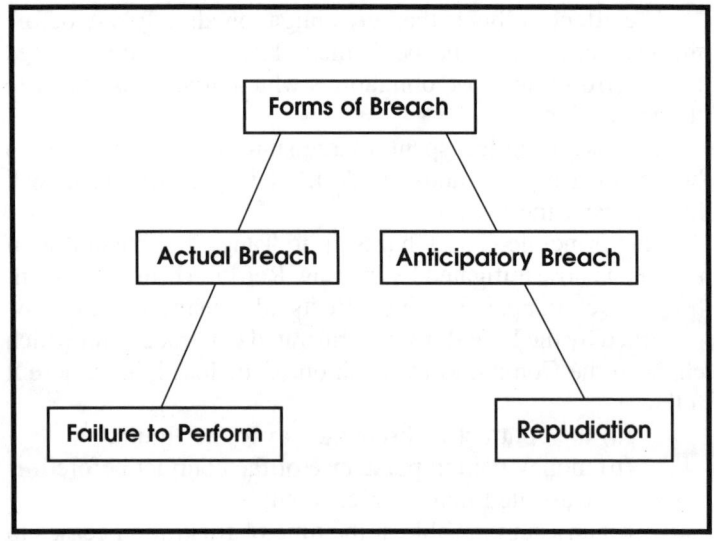

6. Discharge by Breach

A contract may be discharged if there is a breach by one of the parties.

A breach of contract will occur where
— a party fails to perform on the date fixed for performance (called actual breach) or
— indicates an intention not to perform his obligation before the date fixed for performance (called anticipatory breach).

(a) Actual Breach

A contract does not automatically terminate. The innocent party has the right to affirm the contract or treat it as repudiated.

If there is a breach of condition (see Chapter 7—Terms of Contract), ie, a term which goes to the root of the contract, the injured party can treat the contract as discharged and also sue for damages. The injured party may however prefer to treat the contract as still continuing despite a breach of condition and merely claim damages for his loss.

If there is a breach of warranty, the injured party cannot treat the contract as discharged. He can only sue for damages.

(b) Anticipatory Breach

Anticipatory breach means a breach which occurs before the date of performance laid down in the contract. Suppose Tang contracts to sell his house to Tay on a certain day. Before the day of performance, Tang tells Tay that he will not sell the house. Tay may accept the repudiation and sue for damages. He may, at his option, allow the contract to continue until there is an actual breach. The party guilty of anticipatory breach may change his mind and perform the contract after all.

Hochster v De La Tour[14]

T engaged H as a courier to accompany him on a European tour commencing on 1 June. On 11 May, T wrote to H to say that he no longer required his services. On 22 May, H commenced legal proceedings for breach of contract. T objected that there was no actionable breach until 1 June.
Held: H was entitled to sue as soon as the anticipatory breach occurred on 11 May.

Avery v Bowden[15]

A contract to charter a ship to load grain at Odessa within a period of 45 days. The ship arrived at Odessa and the charterer told the master that he did not propose to load a cargo. The master remained at Odessa hoping that the charterer would change his mind. Before the 45 days for loading cargo had expired the outbreak of the Crimean War discharged the contract by frustration.
Held: the shipowner through the master had waived his right to discharge for anticipatory breach with a claim for damages. The contract continued and had been discharged later by frustration (war) without liability on either party.

If the innocent party elects to treat the contract as still in force despite the other party's anticipatory breach, the former may continue with his preparations for performance and recover

14. (1853) 2 E.& Il. 678
15. (1885) 5 E. & Il 714

the agreed price for his services. But any claim for damages will be assessed on the basis of what the plaintiff has really lost.

White & Carter (Councils) v McGregor[16]
M contracted with WC for advertising of M's business. M wrote to cancel the contract but WC elected to advertise as agreed and claimed the agreed payment.
Held: the contract continued in force and WC might recover the agreed price for their services.

The Mihalis Angelos[17]
Charter of a ship to be "ready to load at Haiphong" in Vietnam on 1 July 1965. The charterers had the option to cancel if the ship was not ready to load by 20 July. On 17 July the charterers repudiated the contract believing wrongly that they were entitled to do so. The shipowners accepted the repudiation and claimed damages. On 17 July the ship was still in Hong Kong and could not have reached Haiphong by 20 July.
Held: the shipowners were entitled only to nominal damages since they would have been unable to perform the contract and the charterers could have cancelled it without liability on 20 July.

16. [1962] A.C. 413
17. [1971] 1 Q.B. 164

14 Remedies for Breach of Contract

Where a contract is broken, the injured party has several courses of action open to him. He can:
— refuse further performance of contract;
— bring an action for damages;
— sue on a quantum meruit;
— sue for specific performance;
— sue for injunction.

1. Refusal of Further Performance
If there is a breach of contract, the injured party can treat the contract as discharged and refuse further performance.

2. Damages
Where there is a breach of contract, the usual remedy is to sue for damages. The object of awarding damages for breach of contract is to put the injured party, in so far as money can do it, in the same position as if the contract had been performed.

The injured party can never get more in damages than the loss which he has suffered. Thus, if he suffered no loss and still wins an action, he will get only nominal damages, ie, damages which recognise that he has had his legal right infringed. In a claim for damages, 2 issues arise:
— Remoteness of damages (What consequences shall be compensated for?); and
— Measure of damages (How shall the damages be quantified?).

Contract Law

3. Remoteness of Damage

Remoteness of damage, ie, how far down the sequence of cause and effect should the consequences of breach be traced before they become so indirect that they should be ignored.

Under the famous rule in Hadley v Baxendale,[1] damages may only be awarded in respect of loss which either:
(i) arises naturally, ie, according to the usual course of things for the breach; or
(ii) which the parties may be reasonably supposed to have contemplated in making the contract as the probable result of the breach of it.

Hadley v Baxendale[1]
H owned a mill at Gloucester, which came to a standstill because the main driving shaft had broken. H made a contract with B, a carrier, for the transport of the broken shaft to the makers at Greenwich to serve as a pattern for making a new shaft. Delivery was to be made at Greenwich on the following day. Owing to neglect by B, delivery was delayed and the mill was out of action for a longer period than would have resulted if there had been no delay. B did not know that the mill would be idle during this interval. He was merely aware that he had to transport a broken millshaft from H's mill. H claimed for loss of profits of the mill during the period of delay.
Held: the claim must fail since B did not know that the mill would be idle until the new shaft was delivered (ie, part ii of the Hadley v Baxendale's rule did not apply) and it was not a natural consequence of delay in transport of a broken shaft that the mill would be out of action meanwhile, (ie, part of the rule did not apply). The importance of the shaft was not obvious; the miller might have a spare.

Under the first part of the rule, the defendant is deemed to expect any normal consequence which any other person might also expect; such things are the natural and ordinary consequ-

---

1. (1854) 9 Exch. 341

ences. If the consequence of breach for which damages are claimed is abnormal, ie, what one would not ordinarily expect, the defendant is liable only if he knew in making the contract of the special circumstances from which the abnormal consequence of breach could arise.

Victoria Laundry (Windsor) v Newman Industries,[2]

N contracted to sell a large boiler to V "for immediate use" in U's business of launderers and dyers. Owing to an accident in dismantling the boiler at its previous site, delivery was delayed for 4 months. V claimed damages for (i) normal loss of profits (£16 per week) for the period of delay and (ii) loss of abnormal profits (£262 per week) from losing "highly lucrative" dyeing contracts to be undertaken if the boiler had been delivered on time.

Held: damages for loss of normal profits were recoverable since in the circumstances, failure to deliver major industrial equipment ordered for immediate use would be expected to prevent operation of the plant, ie, it was a natural consequence covered by the first half of the rule. The claim for loss of special profits fell under the second half of the rule. It failed because N had no knowledge of the dyeing contracts and the abnormal profits which they would yield.

The Heron II (Czarnikow v Koufos)[3]

Contract for the shipment of a bulk cargo of sugar from the Black Sea to Basra in Iraq. K, the shipowner, was aware that C were sugar merchants but he did not know that C intended to sell the cargo as soon as it reached Basra. The ship arrived 9 days late and in that time the price of sugar on the market in Basra had fallen. C claimed damages for the loss due to the fall in market value of the cargo over the period of delay.

Held: the claim succeeded. It is common knowledge that the market value of commodities fluctuates so that delay might cause loss. It was sufficiently obvious that

2. [1949] 2 K.B. 528
3. [1969] 1 A.C. 350

a bulk cargo of sugar owned by merchants was destined for sale to which the market value would be relevant.

H Parsons (Livestock) v Uttley Ingham[4]
Contract for the supply and installation at a pig farm of a large storage hopper to hold pig food. Owing to negligence of the supplier the ventilation cowl, sealed during transit to the farm, was left closed. The pig food went mouldy. Young pigs contracted a rare disease from which they died. The pig farmer claimed damages for (i) the value of the dead pigs and (ii) loss of profits from selling the pigs when mature.
Held: the illness of the pigs was to be expected as a natural consequence (ie, the first half of the rule applied). Since illness was to be expected, death from illness, although not a normal consequence, was not too remote. The claim for loss of future profits was too remote and must fail.

4. Measure of Damages

As a general rule the amount awarded as damages is what is needed to put the plaintiff in the position he would have achieved if the contract had been performed. If there is an available market for the goods, the market rule will apply to the sale of goods, ie, the loss is quantified by reference to the market.

Suppose there is failure to deliver goods at a contract price of $100 per ton and at the due time for delivery similar goods are obtainable at a market price of $110 per ton, damages are calculated at the rate of $10 per ton. That is, the difference between the market price and contract price at the time the goods ought to have been delivered.

In a recent case of Jarvis v Swan Tours, damages had been recovered for mental distress where that was the main result of the breach. But it is uncertain how far the Court will develop this new concept.

---

4. [1978] Q.B. 791

Jarvis v Swan Tours[5]
Contract for holiday accommodation at a winter sports centre. What was provided was much inferior to the description given in the defendant's brochure. Damages on the basis of financial loss only were assessed at £32. *Held:* the damages should be increased to £125 to compensate for disappointment and distress.

5. Speculative Damages

The quantification of damages may be very difficult. But the Court will not be deterred by the difficulty or need to speculate from making damages award. The fact that damages are difficult to assess does not prevent the injured party from recovering.

Chaplin v Hicks[6]
H advertised a beauty competition, by which readers of certain newspapers were to select 50 ladies, from among whom H himself would select 12 and for whom he would provide theatrical engagements. C was one of the 50, and, by H's breach of contract, she was not present when the final selection was made.
Held: although it was problematic whether she would have been one of the selected 12, and although it was difficult to assess damages, C was entitled to have the damages assessed.

6. Mitigation

Where there is a breach and if the injured party accepts the breach as discharging the contract, he must take all reasonable steps to mitigate (ie, reduce) the loss occasioned by the breach.

Suppose Tang refuses to deliver goods due on 5 June. Tay must go into the market at once to buy replacement goods. If Tay waits unreasonably until 5 July and the market price has risen, Tay will not receive in damages the difference between contract price and the 5 July price but only between the contract price and the 5 June price.

The injured party is not however expected to act with lightning speed and accept any offer that comes along or to

---

5. [1973] Q.B. 233
6. [1911] 2 K.B. 786

embark on some difficult course to mitigate his loss.

Pilkington v Wood[7]

P instructed a solicitor to act for him in the purchase of a house. The solicitor negligently advised P that the title to the house was good. There was a breach of contract which led to many unfortunate results. The solicitor argued that P should have mitigated his loss by taking legal proceedings against the vendor for having conveyed a defective title. The judge rejected this argument and held that the duty to mitigate did not oblige P to "embark on a complicated and difficult piece of litigation against a third party".

7. Liquidated Damages

Parties may provide in their contract that a specified sum (called liquidated damages) shall be payable in the event of a breach. In construction contracts, for example, it is usual to provide that if the building contractor is in breach of contract by late completion, he shall pay damages of $100 per day. This is a genuine pre-estimate of loss.

Where there is an agreed damages clause in the contract, the plaintiff can recover the specified sum although his actual loss may be less. And if his actual loss is more than the specified sum he can still only recover the specified sum.

The "liquidated damages" clause may be challenged on the grounds that it is a "penalty", ie, a threat held over the head of a party to try to force him to perform the contract. If the court holds that the clause is a penalty clause it is disregarded and the plaintiff cannot recover more than his actual loss. A contract term designed as a penalty to discourage breach is not enforceable. The Court will disregard it and require the injured party to prove the amount of his loss. Thus whether the sum stipulated is recoverable depends on whether it is classified by the Court as:

— a penalty (irrecoverable); or
— liquidated damages (recoverable).

7. [1953] Ch. 770

The principles for distinguishing between the two have been stated by Lord Dunedin in Dunlop Pneumatic Tyre Co Ltd v New Garage & Motor Co Ltd.[8] These are:
  (a) The fact that the payment is described in the contract as a "penalty" or as "liquidated damages" is relevant but not decisive;
  (b) It will be held to be a penalty if the sum stipulated is extravagantly greater than the damage which could conceivably follow from breach;
  (c) It will be held to be a penalty if the breach consists only in not paying a sum of money, and the sum stipulated is greater than the sum which ought to have been paid;
  (d) There is a rebuttable presumption that it is a penalty when "a single lump sum is made payable on the occurrence of one or more or all of several events, some of which may occasion serious, and other but trifling, damage";
  (e) It does not prevent a sum stipulated from being a genuine pre-estimate of damage if the consequences of the breach are such as to make precise pre-estimation almost an impossibility. On the contrary, it is just the situation when it is probable that pre-estimated damage was the true bargain between the parties.

Dunlop v New Garage & Motor Co[9]
The contract for sale of tyres to a garage imposed a minimum retail price (resale price maintenance was then legal). The contract provided that £5 per tyre should be paid by the buyer if he re-sold at less than the prescribed retail price or in 4 other possible cases of breach of contract. He did sell at a lower price and argued that £5 per tyre was a "penalty" and not a genuine pre-estimate of loss.
Held: as a general rule, when a fixed amount is to be paid as damages for breaches of different kinds, some more serious in their consequences than others, that is

8. [1915] A.C. 79
9. supra.

not a genuine pre-estimate of loss and so it is void as a "penalty". But the general rule is merely a presumption which does not always determine the result. In this case, the formula was an honest attempt to agree on liquidated damages and would be upheld.

8. Quantum Meruit

Where the contract makes no express provision for remuneration and there is a breach of contract, the injured party can claim on a *quantum meruit* (ie, as much as he has deserved or earned).

De Bernardy v Harding[10]
> DB agreed to advertise and sell tickets for H who was erecting stands for spectators to view the funeral of the Duke of Wellington. H cancelled the arrangement with DB without justification.
> *Held:* DB might recover from H the value of services rendered.

9. Specific Performance

The Court may in its discretion order the defendant to perform his part of the contract instead of letting him buy himself out of it by paying damages for breach. Specific performance is an order of the Court ordering the defendant to perform a promise that he has made.

Specific performance is an equitable remedy and is discretionary, ie, granted at the discretion of the Court. It is not obtainable, as damages is, as of right. The Court will grant specific performance where it is just and equitable.

No Specific Performance if Damages are Adequate

Specific performance is available only where damages are inadequate. In other words, specific performance will only be ordered in a case where the common law remedy of damages is inadequate. Thus specific performance is rarely ordered of a contract for sale of goods. But specific performance may be ordered of sale of specific goods which are rare and unique and are not available in the market, eg, antiques. Specific

---

10. (1853) 8 Exch. 822

performance is usually granted in a contract for the sale of land since the plaintiff may need the land for a particular purpose and would not be adequately compensated by damages for the loss of his bargain. He could not obtain another piece of land which is identical.

Contracts Not Specifically Enforceable
(a) Personal Service Contracts
Specific performance will not be ordered of contracts of personal service, because of undue interference with man's personal liberty that he should be compelled to serve a master if he does not wish to.

(b) Contracts Requiring Constant Supervision
Specific performance will not be ordered of contracts of such a nature that require constant supervision by the Court.

Ryan v Mutual Tontine Westminster Chambers Association[11]
The landlords of a flat contracted to provide a porter who was to be constantly in attendance. A man was employed as a resident porter but he rarely attended to his duties. Instead, he employed boys and charwomen to perform his duties while he worked elsewhere as a chef. The Court held that the landlords were in breach of contract but it would not grant specific performance because damages was an adequate remedy and the Court could not supervise to see that the work was properly carried out.

(c) Contracts which Lack Mutuality
Specific performance will not generally be ordered in favour of a party unless the court can order it against him. For example, an infant cannot get specific performance because specific performance cannot be ordered against him.

10. Injunction
Injunction is a decree by the Court ordering a person not to do a certain act. It is an equitable remedy given at the discretion of the Court. Injunction will not be granted unless it is just and

---

11. (1893) 1 Ch. 116

Contract Law

equitable to do so. The remedy is used to enforce a negative restriction of a contract. Thus, injunction can be used to restrain a party from committing a breach of a negative undertaking in a personal service contract, if its effect is merely to encourage and not compel the defendant to perform a positive service.

Warner Bros v Nelson[12]

> N, the film star Bette Davis, agreed to work for a year for WB (film producers) and not, during the year, to work for any other film or stage producer nor "to engage in any other occupation" without the consent of WB. N came to England during the year to work for a British film producer. WB sued for an injunction to restrain N from this work in the UK and N resisted, arguing that if the restriction were enforced she must either work for WB (ie, indirectly it would be an order for specific performance of a contract for personal service, which she should not be made to do) or abandon her livelihood. *Held:* the Court would not make an injunction if it would have the result suggested by N. But WB merely asked for an injunction to restrain N from working for a British film producer. That was one part of the restriction accepted by N under her contract and it was fair to hold her to it to that extent. But the Court would not have enforced the "any other occupation" restraint.

Injunction will not be granted if its effect would be to compel the defendant to do something which he could not have been ordered to do by specific performance.

Page One Records Ltd v Britton[13]

> P ask for an injunction to restrain T from engaging as their manager anyone other than P. Injunction was refused because to grant an injunction would in effect compel T to continue to employ P.

---

12. [1937] 1 K.B. 209
13. [1967] 3 All E.R. 822

15 How to Draft a Contract?

1. General Principles

"He who acts in his own cause has a fool for a client," so says a legal wag.

In drafting contracts it is advisable to go to a lawyer so that you can be safeguarded from the pitfalls of the law and that the document you sign is complete, exact and clear. The lawyer should be able to draft the document in language that is precise and technical though not necessarily easy to follow.

Often you ask that the document be short. It is likely that a lawyer's draft is more comprehensive and more detailed than you expect. The draft may guard against contingencies which are remote or which may not have occurred to you. The draft often deals with more matters than you may have considered necessary.

You are apt to be critical of legal jargon such as "whereas", "hereinafter" and other archaic words or expressions not customarily used in everyday life. The tendency is for contracts and other legal documents to be couched in language more closely resembling normal modern English. Archaic language should be replaced by words in current use. Technical terms must be used where appropriate.

The draftsman's effort is to be both comprehensive and exact and keep within the rules of English grammar. But remember, your first duty is to be exact and clear and brief and if that requires you to split an infinitive do so and leave anyone who pleases to criticise your drafting.

2. Drafting Rules

Davidson in his *Precedents and Forms of Conveyancing*[1] suggests several rules to be applied when drafting a contract.

Rule 1
The first rule is that before you commence your draft, the whole design of it should be conceived.

Rule 2
The second rule is that nothing is to be omitted or admitted at random. Every sentence written should have its intent and meaning clearly expressed. If you are careless and include insignificant matters you may be sure that it will not be intelligible to others. Carelessness and ignorance occasion the verbosity with which legal documents are justly reproached. Necessary results should never be stated. In other words, consequences, inevitably flowing from facts previously mentioned should not be expressed. Therefore, if it be said that X died leaving Y his heir-at-law, it is absurd to add "him surviving", because unless Y survived X he could not be heir-at-law.

Rule 3
The third rule is that the order of the draft contract should be logical.

Rule 4
The fourth rule is that the ordinary and accustomed forms of documents and technical language should be used.

Rule 5
The fifth rule is that legal language should be precise and accurate. Every phrase should have a clear meaning and all the phrases should be so connected as not to give rise to ambiguity. Aim at accuracy. Omit superfluous phrases. Give correct references and adhere strictly to the rules of grammar as by the use of apt words.

---

1. 5th ed by Wright & Darley, vol 1 Chapter II pp 65.

3. Intelligibility of Contract Documents
Even if the above rules are applied in the drafting of a contract it will not necessarily be intelligible to a layman. It should however be so, without sacrificing accuracy and comprehensiveness. In drafting, you must try to imagine every possible combination of circumstances to which your words might apply and every conceivable misinterpretation that might be put on them, and to take precautions. You must not be afraid of repetitions or even of identifying them by "aforesaids". You must avoid every potential grammatical ambiguity, and you must keep your eye on the rules of legal interpretation of and the case-law on the meaning of particular words and choose your phrases to fit them. However, if the subject-matter is complicated the contract must be drafted in a manner which deals properly with the complications.

4. Use of Precedents
Generally, precedents should be used only as a guide. Certain precedents outlining the more common forms, eg, a conveyance or mortgage, may be copied. But others, eg, a will or commercial agreement, should be regarded merely as guides to be altered in order to fit your particular transaction.

5. Drafting in Paragraphs
Legal documents used to be hand-written in one compact mass. Sentences were very long and often the whole document was constructed as a single continuous sentence. The reason for unbroken lines from margin to margin may be to leave no space for a fraudulent addition.

Modern documents often have enough blank spaces which make alteration and addition easier than they used to be.

Documents like old deeds are rare these days. However, it is still not unknown to write a document without a paragraph to break it up. It is also common to use very long sentences even when there are paragraphs in the draft.

A useful aid to clearness of statement is to split a long sentence into short paragraphs. Complexity can be broken down and in place of a single continuous sentence a series of short sentences or passages can be written. These can then be arranged as numbered paragraphs.

6. Use of Descriptive Words

When a name or description of a person or thing or event first occurs in a document it can be given a descriptive word for later reference. This can come immediately after the name or description in brackets and be introduced by the words hereinafter called "..." or in this agreement called "..." or simply called "...". The descriptive word is usually in inverted commas in the definition, the inverted commas being omitted when the word is used later in the document. A modern practice is to place the word in brackets immediately after the expression it is to represent, as in:

> Tang See Chim & Catherine Tay Swee Kian ("the Authors")

7. Habits You Should Avoid

Do Not Use Long Uncommon Words or Long Sentences

Keep to a short simple sentence of short words. However, short sentences cannot always be used in legal documents because technical legal expressions may sometimes have to be used in preference to short sentences.

Use Technical Words Where Appropriate

Do not use short ordinary words if a phrase has a precise legal meaning that cannot be expressed except at some length. For example, in a document such as a will, no one would refrain from writing "residue" or "testamentary expenses". In commercial documents, the ordinary phraseology of business is the appropriate language. For example, in a contract for the purchase of goods from overseas, the expressions "f.o.b." and "c.i.f." would be appropriate without explanation.

In the preparation of documents relating to conveyancing, it will not be wise to use any words other than the technical words that are appropriate. To avoid the appearance of "over-legality" in such documents, you can use the device of paragraphs and sparingly use the words "whereas", "aforesaid", "hereinafter" and other lawyers' terms not used in everyday life.

How to Draft a Contract

Verbosity
Prefer the single comprehensive word or phrase. For example, "lands, tenements and hereditaments" was formerly used. Now it can be simply replaced by "lands". "Tenements" is obsolete and "hereditaments" refers to property which descended to an heir and is now not an appropriate word.

Avoid Archaic Language
The most frequently occurring archaic words are "the said" and "the aforesaid".

If any person is mentioned it has been usual whenever the name occurs again to preface it by the words "the said" or "the aforesaid".

The modern view is that if a person is referred to in a document by name, a subsequent mention of that name, unqualified by "said" or "aforesaid", will be understood as referring to that person, unless a contrary intention appears.

The use of descriptive words does away with the use of "said" and "aforesaid". For instance, if a husband appoints as an executrix of his will "my wife Catherine", it is an irritation to the reader to call her, whenever she is named later in the will, "my said wife Catherine"; for "my wife Catherine" can refer to no other person than the wife already named. Similarly, if a date, say 5th June, 1932, has to be mentioned again in the document, no greater clarity is achieved by writing "the said 5th June, 1932".

If there is a recital to a contract, the best way is to use an introductory "whereas", followed by numbered paragraphs.

Words such as "hereinbefore, hereinafter, hereafter", thereof thereto should not be used except when they are clearly the best words. These words, if carefully used, can be an aid to exact expression. But sometimes they may be affected with uncertainty. It is not wise to have too many of them.

You should not use such antique words as "hath agreed", "do hereby grant", when they can be simply written "has agreed", "hereby grant".

Use Punctuation
A frequent complaint of clients is that lawyers do not insert full stops to aid understanding of their meaning. It is obvious

that in a long sentence, commas, colons, semi-colons and brackets will make the meaning clearer.

If a long sentence has to be written, it is best to insert full stops and brackets to aid the eye.

Brackets may also be used as a convenient aid in interpolating an additional statement. For example; "No alteration shall be made that will in the opinion of the Authority (whose decision shall be final) substantially prejudice the rights or interests of any person in respect of any payment already made."

A word of caution in the use of brackets and punctuation marks, especially commas. Stops are little things which may be thought unimportant in the original draft and be omitted in copying. If you use brackets, do not forget to close them. You can always declare that punctuation marks and brackets are part of a document but if you do this you must be very careful that there are no errors in punctuation or brackets in the signed document. Consider the following sentence: "No price too dear." A simple comma gives it an entirely different meaning: "No, price too dear."

8. Schedules

The use of schedules may make a document easier to read. For example, in an employment contract, the duties to be performed by an employee can be neatly set out in a schedule attached to the agreement. This will make the agreement uncluttered and easier to read. An example of this appears in the Appendix.

9. Check Your Draft

However careful you may be you are likely to make an occasional mistake. You can take some safeguards. First, put aside a finished draft for at least a day and you may then find faults you did not notice when you first wrote it. The best way is to have it considered and checked from end to end by someone else.

Do not make errors in matters of fact. It only requires simple checking of figures, names, places and the like. So do check carefully.

10. Specimen Agreement

A specimen agreement—an employment agreement—appears in the Appendix. An agreement first states the parties to the agreement, their descriptions and addresses.

This is followed by what is known as the recital, giving the reasons why the agreement is made. Then comes the main body of the agreement, in law called the habendum.

In the specimen, the habendum states the terms for the employment of Jeffrey Au-Yong by Crystal International Pte Ltd. The duties of the employee are set out in a schedule. This will not make the agreement unnecessarily cluttered and difficult to follow. Finally, the parties sign the agreement. This part of the agreement is called the attestation.

Now that you know all about agreements, you may want to try your hand at one. But please remember the advice given at the beginning of this chapter: when in doubt, consult your lawyer.

Specimen Agreement

Parties

THIS AGREEMENT is made the 7th day of September 1986 Between CRYSTAL INTERNATIONAL PTE LTD a company incorporated in Singapore and having its registered office at 1 New Industrial Road, Singapore 1953 (hereinafter called "the Company") of the one part and JEFFREY AU-YONG (NRIC No. 12345671A) of 102 Battery Road, Singapore 0104 (hereinafter called "the Manager") of the other part.

Recital

WHEREAS:
(1) The Company is engaged in the book publishing business and requires a person with the necessary qualifications and experience to manage its business.
(2) The Manager has the necessary qualifications and experience in the management of a book publishing business.
(3) The Company has agreed to employ the Manager and the Manager has agreed to serve the Company on the terms and conditions hereinafter appearing.

Habendum

NOW IT IS HEREBY AGREED as follows:
1. The Company shall employ the Manager and the Manager shall serve the Company as manager of the Company's business on book publishing for a period of three years commencing on the 1st day of October 1986, subject nevertheless to termination as hereinafter provided.
2. During the period of his employment the Manager undertakes to perform the duties detailed in the schedule to this Agreement.

Habendum

3. The Manager shall be paid a salary of $5,000 per month payable in arrears on the last day of every month.
4. This Agreement may be terminated by either party giving to the other three months' notice in writing.

    IN WITNESS whereof the parties hereto have set their hand the day and year first above written.

Schedule

THE SCHEDULE ABOVE REFERRED TO

Duties of the Manager

1. To manage, maintain and promote the business of the Company.
2. To attend personally during the usual hours of business and to supervise and control the business and to be accessible to the customers and employees of the company.
3. To keep the usual books of account.
4. To pay daily all moneys received in the business into the Company's bank account.
5. Generally to protect the interests of the Company.

Attestation

SIGNED by JOHN SOH   )
for and on behalf of   )
CRYSTAL INTERNATIONAL   )
FTE LTD in the presence of:)

SIGNED by JEFFREY AU-YONG   )
in the presence of:)

The Authors

Catherine Tay Swee Kian is an Advocate and Solicitor of the Supreme Court of Singapore, a barrister, an author and a Senior Lecturer in Business Law at the Faculty of Business Administration, National University of Singapore (NUS).

Miss Tay studied law at Queen Mary College, University of London and graduated with a Bachelor of Laws with Honours (1977) and a Master of Laws (1979), specialising in company, shipping and insurance laws. She was called to the English Bar by Lincoln's Inn in 1978. She did her pupillage under the Honourable Lady Mary Hogg in London and with the law firm of Rodyk and Davidson in Singapore until she was called to the Singapore Bar in 1980.

In 1980 she joined the School of Accountancy in NUS as a Lecturer in Law and currently conducts MBA programmes at the Post-graduate School of Management, NUS. She was also a Legal Consultant to ABN Bank, Singapore.

In February 1984 and July 1986, she made representations to the Parliamentary Select Committee on the Companies (Amendment) Bills 1984 and 1986.

Her publications include *Company Formation Practice Manual*; *Bankruptcy – The Law and Practice*; *Directors' Duties and Liabilities*; *Your Rights as a Consumer*; *Judicial Management*; *A Law Handbook For Businessmen*; *Hotel and Catering Law*; *Have You Made Your Will?*; *Investing in Stocks and Shares*; *Buying and Selling Your Property*; *How to Collect Your Debts and Investing in HDB Property*. Miss Tay has contributed articles to international refereed journals such as the (UK) *Journal of Business Law*, the (UK) *Company Lawyer* as well as the journals of both the Singapore and Hong Kong Law Societies. She has presented papers at many conferences and seminars on company and bankruptcy laws. She is an examiner on law subjects for a number of professional bodies in Singapore and abroad and conducts seminars for banks, statutory boards, hotels, corporations, clubs and associations.

Tang See Chim studied law in London and was called to the Bar by the Middle Temple in 1955. He graduated with a Bachelor of Science in Economics with Honours in 1962 from the London School of Economics, University of London.

He has been Parliamentary Secretary, Ministry of Finance (1968–70), Minister of State for Finance (1970–72), Deputy Speaker of Parliament (1972–81) and Member of Parliament (1966–88). He was a member of the Parliamentary Select Committee on the Companies Bill, 1967. He was also a member of the Parliamentary Select Committee on the recent Companies (Amendment) Bill, 1986.

He is the co-author (with Catherine Tay Swee Kian) of *Your Rights as a Consumer*. Mr Tang is a legal practitioner and a partner in the law firm of Rodyk and Davidson.

Index

ACCEPTANCE
  absolute and unqualified 24
  by post 28
  instantaneous contracts 27
  communication of 27
  cross-offers 29
  counteroffer 25
  subject to contract 30

ACCORD AND SATISFACTION
  definition 40
  discharge of contract 40

BREACH OF CONTRACT
  anticipatory 110-112
  damages, give rise to action for 113
  injunction 122
  mitigation 117
  quantum meruit 120
  specific performance 120

CAPACITY TO CONTRACT
  corporations 48, 51
  mentally disordercd and drunken persons 52
  minors 48
  necessaries 49
  void contracts 50
  voidable contracts 50

COMFORT LETTERS 34

COMMON MISTAKE 83

CONDITIONS
  breach, of 56, 57
  meaning of 56,57

CONSIDERATION
  adequacy 37
  executed 36
  executory 36

  insufficiency of 37
  part payment of debt 39-40
  past 35, 38
  Rule in Pinnel's ease 39

CONTRACT
  correspondence constituting, 26

CROSS-OFFERS
  whetber agreement may result from 30

DAMAGES
  adequacy 120-121
  liquidated 118
  measure of 116
  mitigation 117
  quantum meruit 120
  remoteness of damage 114
  speculative 117

DEBT
  part payment 39-40
  Pinnel's Case 40

DISCHARGE OF CONTRACTS
  acceptance of partial performance 103
  actual breacb 110
  agreement, by 104
  anticipatory breach 110-111
  breach, by 109
  divisible contracts 102
  frustration 105,107,108
  performance, by 101
  substantial performance 104

DOMESTIC AGREEMENTS
  generally 31-33

DRAFTING OF CONTRACT
  archaic language 127
  checking draft 128
  descriptive words 126

133

drafting in paragraphs 125
intelligibility 125
precedents, use of 125
technical words 126
verbosity 127

DURESS
economic duress 79-80
fiduciary relationship 80
threat of force 79
undue influence distinguished from 79-80

ESTOPPEL
meaning of 41
promissory estoppel 41-42

EXECUTED CONSIDERATION
see Consideration

EXECUTORY CONSIDERATION
see Consideration

EXEMPTION CLAUSES
fundamental breach 64-65
judicial restrictions 59
statutory restrictions 63

FORMALITIES OF CONTRACT
contracts evidenced in writing 44
contracts under seal or by deed 43
written contracts 43-44

FRAUDULENT MISREPRESENTATION
see Misrepresentation

FRUSTRATION
doctrine of 105
limits to 107
self-induced,
party cannot rely on 107

GAMING
definition 92

ILLEGAL CONTRACTS
common law, illegal at 92
consequences of illegality 94-95
contracts in restraint of trade 96
contract of employment 97
contract of sale of business 99
excessive area 95
defraud revenue 94
pari delicto 95
public safety, contracts prejudicial to 93
sexually immoral contracts 93
solus trading agreements 99-100
tort, crime, contract to commit 92
void contracts
by public policy 96
by statute 96

INTENTION
commercial agreements 33-34
domestic social agreements 31-33
legal relations to create 31

INVITATION TO TREAT
instances of 20-I
offer distinguished from 20
shop, goods exposed for sale in 21

LEGAL RELATIONS
intention to create 31

LIQUIDATED DAMAGES
see Damages

LOAN
minors 48,50
necessaries 49,50

MEASURE OF DAMAGES
see Damages

134

MISREPRESENTATION
    exemption clauses 78
    fraudulent 72
    Hedley Byrne case 73
    inducement 70
    innocent 75
    Misrepresentation Act 74
    negligent 73
    rescission 75
    restitution and indemnity 75-76
    silence as 69
    statement of fact 67
    types of 91

MISTAKE
    common 83
    mistake over documents 89
    mutual 85-86
    non est factum 89-90
    unilateral 86

MITIGATION OF DAMAGES
    see Damages

MUTUAL MISTAKE
    see Mistake

OFFER
    communication of 22
    invitation to treat distinguished from 20
    lapse of 23
    rejection of 23
    revocation of 22

PART PAYMENT 30

PAST CONSIDERATION
    see Consideration

PENALTY
    liquidated damages distinguished 118-120

PROMISSORY ESTOPPEL
    doctrine of 41

QUANTUM MERUIT
    see Damages

RECTIFICATION
    common intention 91
    mistake, on grounds of, generally 91

REMEDIES
    breach of contract, for 113
    damages 113
    injunction 122
    liquidated damages 118
    measure of damages 116
    mitigation 117
    personal service contracts 121
    quantum meruit 120
    refusal of further performance 113
    remoteness of damage 114
    specific performance 120
    speculative damages 117

REMOTENESS OF DAMAGE
    see Damages

RESCISSION 72, 75, 76

RESTITUTION 75

RESTRAINT OF TRADE 96, 97

SOLUS AGREEMENT 99

SPECIFIC PERFORMANCE 120

STANDARD FORM CONTRACTS 58

SUFFICIENCY
    consideration of 37

135

TERMS OF CONTRACT
  complex 57
  conditions and warranties 56
  express 54
  implied 55
  parol evidence rule 54
  representations distinguished from 53

UNDUE INFLUENCE
  effect of 79-80
  relationship existing between parties 78

UNILATERAL MISTAKE
  see Mistake

VOID CONTRACT
  minor, of, generally 50
  mistake 87
  wagering contracts 92

VOIDABLE CONTRACT
  minor of 48, 50

WARRANTIES
  breach, of 56-57
  meaning of 56-57